FOREWORD BY

FINANCIAL

CPR.

7 STEPS TO AVOID A FINANCIAL CRISIS

JAMES L. PARIS
AND
J.W. DICKS

CREATION HOUSE
BOOKS ABOUT SPIRIT-LED LIVING
ORLANDO, FLORIDA

Creation House
Strang Communications Company
600 Rinehart Road
Lake Mary, FL 32746

In loving memory of my nephew,
Carmen Paris. Although we
had a brief time to share,
he will always be remembered.
— Jim

To my mother,
who taught me Jesus loves me,
and to Buddy and Becky,
who helped me remember.
— J. W.

CONTENTS

FINANCIAL CRISIS has become an American reality. Many of our parents or grandparents suffered through a national crisis of mammoth proportions, the Great Depression. Today their children and grandchildren endure more private financial depressions of their own.

Private, but no less personally agonizing.

I've talked to many such people in my years of doing the national "Point of View" radio talk show. The booby traps in today's world seem endless: crushing debt, business failure, loss of a job, insurance problems, illness. The casualties are mounting. Some people just got caught in circumstances beyond their control. Others admit they made mistakes, misjudgments or unwise decisions, but now they are ready to follow new beginnings and a fresh path.

That's what I like about *Financial CPR*. This is a book about new beginnings and fresh paths for those who are truly "at the end of themselves" and ready to follow a higher wisdom. With an eye-opening mixture of expertise, sensitivity and straight talk, I believe James Paris, a premier financial counselor, and J. W. Dicks, an attorney with twenty-two years of experience in financial industries and chairman of the board for a major investment advisory company, have written *the* handbook for recovery from financial crisis. Yes, this is a spiritual book, based on the precepts of the Bible. But make no mistake, *Financial CPR* is as practical and helpful a financial book as you will find in any bookstore. In fact, if it's practical help you're looking for, I suspect this book will be better than any.

You see, I've witnessed James Paris as he has talked with worried and often hurting men and women. As a guest on "Point of View," he has sat at our microphones and helped caller after caller scramble out of the surf of financial despair and onto the solid rock of hope. And if he can do so much for people in a brief phone call, I'm excited to imagine what an entire book will do for you!

My second reason for confidence is that I've read other books by James Paris and have seen their impact. His materials continue to be one of the most in-demand resources I've ever publicly mentioned. The reason? They work! James Paris is a *solid, reliable* financial counselor who avoids destructive fads and fantasies so often waiting for the gullible. In fact, I recommend his "recovery methods" to the victims of these very schemes. The prevalence of *unsound* financial counseling is all the more reason for a *sound* book like this one.

How will you deal with your financial crisis? Will you allow it to defeat you? Will you ignore its message and plunge into further trouble? Or, instead, will you allow your crisis to teach you something valuable about mastering godly, practical wisdom as you travel the path of sound advice back to stability?

If you take the pages of this book to heart, I'm convinced you'll one day see your struggle as a blessing. It's certain that you will be a stronger, more secure person. Your financial crisis is not a curse but a challenge. I commend you for putting yourself under the care of two advisors such as these as you summon your strength to meet this challenge head-on.

Marlin Maddoux
President of
International Christian Media
and USA Radio Network

AS WE write this book, the country has just completed another presidential election. The key to its victory was clearly the people's belief that Bill Clinton had better plans for the country's economic future and, consequently, theirs too.

Throughout the election each candidate had attempted to woo voters with his version of America's, and their, financial solutions. Unfortunately, none of them was right.

Financial disease, like all maladies, has at its roots the sins of man. The cure to both is likewise the same. It is found not within us but in Christ, who lives within us.

The purpose of this book is simple. We want to show you that there is a formula to cure all of life's financial problems. If you follow the formula, you will find the answers you need.

Before you interpret this statement as either cavalier or naive, let us state that it was not meant to imply that your financial problems are easy. On the contrary, that is not the nature and purpose of human life. Our problems, financial or otherwise, are part of our very mission. What we do mean is that there is a process you can use with any financial problem you face. If you are loyal to the process, the solution will be yours even though the path along the journey may be rocky.

In the opening chapter of this book, we share with you a formula we believe has been given to all of us as a prescription to cure our problems.

In subsequent chapters we break down each part of the formula so that you can see how it fits together. Just like medicine for any disease, you can't skip part of the prescription and expect the desired results. You must go step by step, slowly and deliberately.

Finally, in very practical terms, we explain how the formula can be used to solve today's major financial problems, including your own. To do this we call upon our own skill and background and the talents we have been given to apply the formulas.

Ultimately, it is our wish that you not only learn the formula and how to use it in the situations we present, but that you realize it can be used in any financial situation. Once you understand, we hope you will be comfortable applying this form of CPR wherever you see a financial crisis.

ONE

THE SECRET OF THE FIRST MIRACLE

THE FIRST miracle of Jesus has been a puzzle to many. Compared to other miracles performed, the events at the wedding in Cana were certainly insignificant. There was no raising of the dead. There was no healing. There was not even a dismissal of evil spirits. Jesus simply turned water into wine.

We also know, however, that Jesus taught in parables. He let the true meanings in the lessons He taught reveal themselves only when a person was ready to understand.

Would it be any surprise that this miracle might disclose to us something more than the event itself? We think not. In fact, we think it significant that one of the things the miracle teaches may well be one of the most important lessons we must learn in order to survive: how to solve problems.

Let us review this simple story and highlight the miracle lesson we may learn from it.

It is two days into Jesus' evangelistic mission. He has spoken with John the Baptist and has chosen His twelve disciples.

On this day there is a break in the spiritual events. There is to be a wedding. We don't know whose wedding it is, but certainly it must have been a close friend, for not only was Jesus and His family invited, but also His disciples.

Whether the addition of Jesus' disciples created an extra burden on the festival or whether the host had simply not planned properly for the event, we do not know. However, we are told in John 2 that a problem came up. In the middle of the wedding festival the host ran out of wine.

If you've ever been in a similar situation, where you have all your friends over for a special occasion and you run out of food or drink, you know it can be embarrassing. This would be especially true at your daughter's wedding. Somehow Mary, the mother of Jesus, heard there was a problem. Perhaps the mother of the bride came to Mary, worried about the refreshments. What were they to do?

> On the third day a wedding took place at Cana in Galilee. Jesus' mother was there, and Jesus and his disciples had also been invited to the wedding. When the wine was gone, Jesus' mother said to him, "They have no more wine" (John 2:1-3).

11

In our lives, as in the life of Jesus, we are often called to face problems which occur without warning. Here were Mary and Jesus in a very common setting, attending a wedding with family and friends, and an unexpected problem arose.

Could this happen to you?

How many times have you been going about your life when at the least expected moment you were faced with a problem?

How did you handle the situation?

Did you become emotionally upset, unable to face the task at hand?

Often this is the case. Many people attempt to avoid problems by refusing to face them. They hope they will go away. Unfortunately, life doesn't work that way. In fact, learning to deal with problems is the very essence of what life is all about. The better we get at solving problems, the more problems we are given to handle, always under God's promise never to lay more on us than we can bear.

> "Dear woman, why do you involve me?" Jesus replied. "My time has not yet come" (John 2:4).

Jesus speaks straight to His mother. He is surprised. Just as we find ourselves in difficult times, He was not expecting to face this type of problem. We rarely are either. From the tone of His response, we can tell He was rattled, but He didn't stay rattled long. Instead, He addressed the problem at hand quickly, realizing that whether or not the time was appropriate, someone needed to take charge of the situation.

How did Mary react? Even before Jesus acted,

Mary spoke quickly and directly to the servants: "Do whatever he tells you" (John 2:5).

Mary was confident that her son could solve the problem. Her confidence took control of the situation, and she immediately implemented a plan of action.

Nearby stood six stone water jars, the kind used by the Jews for ceremonial washing, each holding from twenty to thirty gallons.

Jesus said to the servants, "Fill the jars with water"; so they filled them to the brim (John 2:6-7).

Notice all of this action. Mary said, "Get ready." Jesus said, "Fill these jars." The servants not only filled the jars, but they filled them to the top.

Does this seem a little strange? No one is wringing his hands or wondering what to do. No one is doing his job halfheartedly. The servants take jars that can hold twenty to thirty gallons of water and fill them to the top. They must have been very heavy, but no one complained or thought they shouldn't fill them all the way. No, not this group. They filled them to the top.

Then he told them, "Now draw some out and take it to the master of the banquet" (John 2:8).

What do you think the servants are thinking? Put yourself in their shoes. You are now going to take some of the water you just poured into a jug and give it to the master of your house, who is probably a bit upset because there is no more wine, and you are going to tell him, "Here is your wine."

What was the servants' reaction?

> They did so, and the master of the banquet tasted the water that had been turned into wine (John 2:8-9).

The servants showed no doubt. They followed the instructions precisely, and all were rewarded for their actions.

This is the story of the first miracle. It is also an example of how we are to solve our problems. Sometimes the problems we face will be simple. Sometimes they will seem almost impossible. Yet what we learn in this first miracle is that the pattern for solving the problem is always the same. There are steps we can follow as closely as any road map. By doing so, we will be guided through unfamiliar territory. Just as the map tells us which direction to go even though we have never been there before, so the principles behind these steps can be used to solve any problem we may face in life.

Step 1: Define the Crisis.

So many of us live our lives in confusion. We don't know how to solve our problems because we don't even know what they are. To find the answers we must first state clearly what the problems are. When Mary told Jesus, "They have no more wine," there was no question what needed to be done.

Step 2: Begin With the End in Mind.

Answers don't simply come about. There are

steps to be taken which lead us to the conclusions we need to reach.

Step 3: Remain Calm.

Don't panic over your problem. Remain calm but keep moving toward a solution.

Step 4: Develop Your Own Success Formula.

You can never get where you're going if you don't know the direction. Research and gather facts; once you have them, develop your own individual success solution.

Step 5: Seek Counsel of the Wise.

Mary did. Even Jesus' mother knew to turn to Him with a problem. Should you expect to do less than the mother of Christ?

Step 6: Remember: All You Can Do Is Enough.

Don't worry about things you can't control. If you could control them, they wouldn't be a problem. If you can't control your circumstances, go to the Father and submit them and yourself to Him.

Step 7: Expect a Miracle.

Just as Mary knew Jesus would meet their needs, you can expect Him to meet yours. A miracle is not just the healing of the sick or the raising of the dead. Like changing water to wine, it is any solution that comes through believing Jesus will keep His promise to those who trust in Him.

These are your seven principles for solving any problem. As Jesus told the servants at the wedding in Cana, "Now draw some out..." (John 2:8).

TWO

DEFINE THE CRISIS

PHYSICAL CPR training is very precise. You must follow it step by step. So is financial CPR. You must always begin at the beginning. Define your crisis.

The difficulty with this comes from the nature of such situations. By definition, if you have a crisis, a lot of unwanted action is going on. Your major task at this point is to sort through the chaos and determine exactly what your problem is. To do so you must eliminate the emotion and the stress so that you can truly see the problem.

A friend of ours recently asked advice about how he should counsel a relative who was having financial difficulties. While explaining the relative's predicament, our friend used the often-quoted line, "I wish this person didn't have such problems. Life is so difficult."

Of course it's difficult. From the time of man's fall from grace, that has been our lot. Life is not easy, and wishing it were so will not make it better. Further, even if we were to take away one set of problems, it is very possible the next burden might be greater. If you doubt this, you have only to look around you. While there are others whose outward lives may look more appealing, are you really willing to trade your problems for theirs? Romans 5:3-4 says:

> Not only so, but we also rejoice in our sufferings, because we know that suffering produces perseverance; perseverance, character; and character, hope.

By examining this truth, we come to the inescapable conclusion that we humans will all have problems, many of which are financial. The joy we experience in life is often based on how we handle the problems we are given. Let us turn our attention to another time. How does Jesus answer the question?

> By this time it was late in the day, so his disciples came to him. "This is a remote place," they said, "and it's already very late. Send the people away so they can go to the surrounding countryside and villages and buy themselves something to eat."

But he answered, "You give them something to eat."

They said to him, "That would take eight months of a man's wages! Are we to go and spend that much on bread and give it to them to eat?" (Mark 6:35-37).

Is this happening in your life now? Has Jesus turned a problem over to you and said, "You solve it"?

Are you answering now with excuses the same way the disciples did? Are you saying, "I can't do that. I don't have enough money"?

Sounds familiar, doesn't it? It should, because we all have said it. We have let the burdens of our present circumstances so overwhelm us that we can't see the answers to our own problems, much less be about the work of helping others. Fortunately for us, we aren't alone. Yes, we may feel alone, we may act alone, but we are not alone.

Jesus didn't leave the disciples helpless and hopeless. He gave them the chance to solve the problem themselves, hoping they would feed the people and handle the situation themselves. But when they didn't, He did not leave them stranded. He showed them how to meet the challenge, just as He shows us how to solve our problems.

"How many loaves do you have?" he asked. "Go and see" (Mark 6:38).

In this verse Jesus takes us through our first step of problem solving. Define the problem. Go and see exactly what you have. Do an accounting.

Frequently, when we describe the nature of the

first step, our listeners will demonstrate their laziness by telling us their problems in vague, general terms.

"I'm so far in debt I'll never get out" is a common excuse used by people under financial stress.

This type of answer is not what you need to solve a financial dilemma. You must be specific. How far in debt are you? How long would it take for you to save that much money? Whom can you go to for help?

How specific did Jesus want His followers to be? He told them to go out among those five thousand people and come back with a report.

What was the disciples' report?

> When they found out, they said, "Five [loaves] — and two fish" (Mark 6:38).

How is that for being specific? Out of five thousand people, they determined the very number of fish and bread the people had.

This is exactly the method we must use to solve problems in our own lives. Before you seek a solution, you must define your problem. You must be specific as to what that problem is. If you aren't, it will be impossible to find a solution to it.

In journalism school we were taught a simple formula for getting to the heart of a news story: 5W+H (Who, What, When, Where, Why and How). Use this same formula in answering questions about your financial problem.

We have known many people with financial difficulties. Some went bankrupt owing millions of dollars. We have known others who owed only a few hundred dollars and still went bankrupt. With regard to the level of personal stress, the problem was equally severe. Unfortunately, help might have come more quickly if those problems had been defined clearly and if help had been sought.

Once you define your problem, what do you do next?

> Then Jesus said to the followers, "Tell all the people to sit in groups on the green grass." So all the people sat in groups of 50 or groups of 100. Jesus took the five loaves and two fish. He looked up to heaven and thanked God for the bread. He divided the bread and gave it to his followers for them to give to the people. Then he divided the two fish among them all. All the people ate and were satisfied. The followers filled 12 baskets with the pieces of bread and fish that were not eaten. There were about 5,000 men there who ate (Mark 6:39-44, Everyday).

We learn four new facts from the rest of this story.

First, we see that every problem contains the key to its own solution.

Jesus and His followers had a food problem. Yet they had some food. You may have a money problem, yet you may have some money or a resource to which you may turn. Look inside the problem itself for ways to solve it.

Second, once we define the crisis we see how to act.

Jesus' instructions were very specific. He broke down the problem (feeding five thousand) into smaller, more manageable proportions (feeding fifty and a hundred) and solved them one at a time. Sometimes problems seem insurmountable simply because of their size. By breaking them down into smaller parts, we can focus on that which is more manageable. The starving poor of Somalia in Africa find it impossible to think about a permanent solution to their food problem. What is more important, however, is for them to solve the problem for today. Once you solve today's problem, you are free to look beyond. However, if you don't solve your problem today, you may never see tomorrow.

From a financial perspective your problem may be, How do I feed myself and my family today? By solving that one smaller problem, you remain able to look for the alternate solution. Just as the Somalis are discovering, tomorrow may be different when they know that food is being flown in today.

Third, we see Jesus' demonstration of thanks for what He had. Few of us are able to see beyond our problems to say a prayer of thanks for what we do have. How can we expect to get more if we are not even thankful for what we have? It seems so simple, yet we are always looking for more — looking on the other side of the mountain.

Fourth, we see the importance of faith in acting out the plan. As we step out in faith, we will not only solve the defined problem, but we will also find an abundance left over. Even after five thousand people were fed from the few loaves of bread and fish, an abundance was left over. Should we expect any less in our own lives? The answer is, of course, no. God has promised us abundant life (John 10:10), but we must have the faith to see that promise come to pass.

THREE

BEGIN WITH THE END IN MIND

O NE OF the keys to problem solving is the ability to *focus* correctly. Whenever most people face problems, they focus on the symptoms. To have a long-term victory over crisis you must have a specific target. To achieve success you must start with specific results you wish to achieve and have a plan to reach your objective.

Every day in the financial world we see people who are classic examples of symptom focusing. One is the man who has been laid off from work and loses touch with the situation. He can't make his mortgage payments. His car needs a minor repair and won't run until it's fixed. His children don't understand why they can't go on an outing with their friends. These are all serious aspects of this man's situation. However, they are not the problem. They are symptoms of his real problem, which is that he is out of work. Solve that problem, bring in more money, and the symptoms will go away.

It is very important to note that no matter what prescription this man uses to relieve the symptoms, until he attacks the problem he will not have a cure. The result is that more symptoms will develop, and the cycle will continue unending. Some people call this being in a rut. In some cases it may even seem like a canyon. Unfortunately, to treat the symptoms is to apply medicine to the wrong thing.

In Luke 14 Jesus gives us two very clear examples of how we are to solve our problems.

> Suppose one of you wants to build a tower. Will he not first sit down and estimate the cost to see if he has enough money to complete it? For if he lays the foundation and is not able to finish it, everyone who sees it will ridicule him, saying, "This fellow began to build and was not able to finish" (Luke 14:28-30).

What clearer picture of problem solving can you get than this? If you want to build a tower, you had better see how much it is going to cost and whether you can afford it. You must plan. You must start with the end, or goal, in mind and work backward, using the following questions.

Problem

1. *What*: I want to build a tower.

2. *How* much money will I need?

   a. How much material will be necessary?

   b. How many people?

   c. How long will it take?

3. *Where* will I build it?

4. *When* do I need to start?

5. *Who* can help me?

6. *Why* do I need this tower?

Do you recognize the formula 5W + H (who, what, when, where, why and how) that we introduced in the first chapter?

Note that the order of the questions is different this time, and that is OK. What we must do is start with the problem and then ask all of the questions. In our earlier example of being unemployed, we might set out our formula this way:

1. *What*: I need a job.

2. *When*: Right now. Thus I realize that my focus is immediate. I don't have time to deal with the symptoms.

3. *Where*: Where am I willing to go? Am I limiting myself to this city? This state?

4. *Why*: I need a job to pay specific bills

that are due.

5. *Who*: Whom do I know that can help?

   a. Friends

   b. People I have worked with

6. *How* can I get a job?

Knowing the problem and learning how to list all the components of it are the important first steps toward the answer. What else does Jesus say to do? In Luke 14:31 He says:

> Or suppose a king is about to go to war against another king. Will he not first *sit down and consider* whether he is able with ten thousand men to oppose the one coming against him with twenty thousand? If he is not able, he will send a delegation while the other is still a long way off and will ask for terms of peace (Luke 14:31-32, italics added).

Has there ever been a more clear directive for planning? Jesus is saying to us that planning is so important that failure to do so can stack us up against incredible odds that would lead to certain defeat. It is our responsibility to do the proper planning to assess those odds and make whatever correction is necessary. We cannot sit back and expect God to do it for us, because He has clearly told us that our job is to find the answers to our own problems. These answers begin with goal setting — having the end in mind from the start.

FOUR

REMAIN CALM

I F YOU have had the opportunity to take a first-aid class, you have heard the statement "In an emergency, always stay calm." If there is one thing during an emergency that people are *not*, it is calm. As you remember from the first miracle, Jesus' mother did not panic when the wine ran out. Yet it seems likely that panicking was probably in order. Rather than focusing on the problem, however, she shifted her focus to a solution.

As we continue to develop your training in financial CPR, we cannot overemphasize the importance of staying calm in your crisis. The reason is simple: You need all of your mental energy to think of solutions to your problem. What does worrying accomplish anyway? The apostle Paul told the Philippians, "Do not be anxious about anything" (4:6). In other words, "Don't worry; be happy."

A recent book observed that 90 percent of what we worry about never happens. After thinking about this, we would have to agree strongly. Yet so many people we meet still play the "what if" game: "What if this happens or that happens?"

We respond as Jesus did: "Don't worry!"

While counseling people who are going through a financial crisis, we often discover that they have created a second crisis through their worrying about the original problem. That's really not such a great action to take in a time of crisis. Imagine trying to give someone CPR and breaking two or three ribs in the process!

One of the most profound stories in Scripture is found in Matthew 8. Jesus and the disciples were in a boat when a terrible storm came up out of nowhere. The situation was serious. Matthew describes the storm as being so bad that the ship was covered with waves; the disciples expected to die.

Together they went to Jesus and found Him sleeping! "Lord, save us! We're going to drown!" they cried in desperation (Matt. 8:25).

Jesus rebuked the wind and the seas, and there was a great calm.

The disciples said among themselves, "What kind of man is this? Even the winds and the waves obey him!" (Matt. 8:27). They still had not realized the deity of Jesus Christ.

A myriad of lessons can be gleaned from this story, but the one most intriguing to us is, how could Jesus be asleep and at the same time the disciples panicking?

We have asked ourselves this question many times as we have seen people react differently in similar situations. The newspapers are filled with stories of desperate people doing desperate things. How tragic to think that thousands of people have committed suicide over financial challenges. To assist in the financial cure we have developed the following four truths about controlling your emotions in a financial crisis.

1. You are not your circumstance.

2. Things are really not that bad.

3. Count your blessings.

4. It's only money.

You Are Not Your Circumstance.

Financial bankruptcy does not mean personal bankruptcy. An individual who is laid off is not a personal failure. As we meet people in their crisis circumstances, it is both interesting and tragic to see how personally traumatized they are by their situation. The problem is simple: They allow themselves and their circumstances to become one.

This dangerous emotional roller coaster is more common among men, but women are not excluded from its damage. When Bill Jones stops being Bill Jones and transforms into Bill Jones "The Bank President," he has set himself up for a fall. If he identifies his self-worth with his profession, he has built his house on sandy soil. Likewise, people who are well off financially see themselves as wealthy individuals. By doing so they link their personal self-worth to their money. Elvis Presley, John Belushi, Marilyn Monroe and countless other financially successful individuals suffered from an identity crisis. They built their houses on sandy soil, and when things got difficult the foundation was unable to withstand the stress.

You must build your life on an identity that *no one* can take from you. Your old identity (the sinful man) has been crucified with Christ, and it is no longer your life but Jesus Christ living through you (Rom. 6:1-14). People who endure crisis are not superhuman; they do, however, allow Jesus Christ to overcome the adversity for them. *Remember, you are not your circumstances.*

> The rain came down, the streams rose, and the winds blew and beat against that house; yet it did not fall, because it had its foundation on the rock (Matt. 7:25).

Things Are Really Not That Bad.

A wise man was once quoted as giving advice to an individual who was experiencing financial adversity. He asked the man, "How important would your problem be if you were told today you had only seven days to live?" This thought-provoking question is one to keep in mind the next time you assess your troubles.

A friend of ours in his mid-twenties who has a wife and a two-year-old daughter was recently diagnosed with terminal cancer. At the moment we heard the news, all of our problems were suddenly dwarfed by the reality that things are not so bad.

On a global scale most Americans don't realize how gladly their foreign counterparts would trade places with them. When your outlook gets gloomy, it's easy to let your emotions take control. The truth is that *things are really not that bad!*

Count Your Blessings.

Most of us have taken our blessings for granted. An old hymn of the church says, "Count your blessings, name them one by one...[and] see what God has done." An interesting tradition practiced by the Israelites was to build an altar to serve as a memory of God's providing a miracle.

Anyone who has had the opportunity to be married to a loving spouse, with a roof over his head and three square meals a day, has plenty to be thankful for. If we were to stop with these blessings, it would be sufficient. Many, if not most, of us have experienced incredible blessings, some beyond belief. One surefire way to rise above your crisis is to sit down in a quiet place and count your blessings. You will conclude, without a doubt, that *God is faithful!*

It's Only Money.

What an absurd thing to write, you might say. The Bible teaches:

> The love of money is a root of all kinds of evil. Some people, eager for money, have wandered from the faith and pierced themselves with many griefs (1 Tim. 6:10).

Another great scripture is Hebrews 13:5:

> Keep your lives free from the love of money and be content with what you have,

because God has said,

"Never will I leave you; never will I forsake you."

What would you be willing to do for money? Many Christians are guilty of being preoccupied with money. Mind you, this includes not just the rich, the poor or the middle class exclusively; rather it includes people from all three groups.

We all know individuals who have had the wrong attitude — people with or without money. God said that Job was a "righteous man" during both his days of wealth and his times of tragedy. Throughout your financial crisis, take a deep breath and say, "It's only money!" This therapeutic advice could cost you several thousand dollars in a good counselor's office, but we offer it *free*.

As we conclude this chapter, we give the following five reasons for not panicking:

1. It doesn't solve your problem.

2. It will make you sick.

3. It is a sin.

4. It will affect your marriage.

5. It drains your energy.

While it is only human and proper to be concerned, overreacting to your crisis is certain to add confusion to the situation. Pray and ask God to help you find relief from your mental anxiety. Despite your situation, we encourage you not to panic; you are only four steps from your solution.

31

FIVE

DEVELOP YOUR OWN SUCCESS FORMULA

A wise man thinks ahead; a fool doesn't, and even brags about it!
                                    Proverbs 13:16, TLB

IT IS interesting to see how much the Bible has to say about planning. To get out of your financial crisis, you must have a plan. Most people we talk with about creating a plan to overcome their crisis say, "I never considered that." For some reason we believe that planning is for building but that rebuilding does not require a plan.

For years we have watched the entertaining television program "MacGyver." It's also a great lesson on problem solving. We are always amazed to see MacGyver escape from near death each episode with a brilliant use of his resources. Whatever the crisis, MacGyver seems to escape unharmed. After watching several episodes you would expect to be bored — but no! MacGyver may be trapped in the back of a shipping truck with a hanger, a bottle of bleach and a ten-speed bike.

How can any of that help? you might ask.

In minutes MacGyver could take apart the bike, use the pipes and bleach to make a bomb, then light a match attached to the end of the unfolded hanger to ignite the explosion to release himself.

Most of us are sitting right now among the resources necessary to solve our problem. The question is: Are we willing to create a plan and use the resources at our disposal to solve the problems we face? Many times the answer is no.

We have published a series of books that have been very well received. The common theme was "the thirty-day quick start." We have offered a thirty-day program on numerous subjects including taxes, investing and even starting a small business. In retrospect, we feel these books were successful because they created a step-by-step plan to accomplish a goal in thirty days. Each day progress is made until after thirty days — success! Just like the old vaudeville joke — "How do you eat an elephant? One bite at a time" — one must solve a crisis one step at a time.

FOUR STEPS TO CREATING YOUR PLAN

1. Prioritize.

2. Create a time line.

3. Create a daily action plan.

4. Monitor the plan.

Prioritize.

As you create your plan, it is very important to prioritize. Most people are guilty of focusing their energies on the urgent rather than the important. Stephen R. Covey, author of *The Seven Habits of Highly Effective People*, lays this concept as the foundation of his book.

The most common example of this conflict is the telephone. Imagine you are getting ready to create your plan to solve your crisis. You are in a quiet place in the house, your mind is focusing and, just as your pencil hits the paper, the telephone rings. What do you do? That's when you jump up and run to the phone and spend twenty minutes warding off a water-purifier salesman. Which was the more important activity, creating your plan or answering the phone?

Interestingly enough, we have observed that the most important activities are often the least urgent. Essentially these high-priority items don't scream for attention. We must not let the urgent take precedence over the important. In just about every crisis we have seen, urgent issues seem to overshadow the important. Don't fall prey to the temptation to become engrossed in trying to solve short-term symptoms of the problem. Go to the real problem and focus your attention.

Create a Time Line.

After determining what is important and developing a plan to address it, the next step is to make a commitment to a schedule to reach your goal. One of the best definitions we have heard for a goal is "a dream with a date for achievement." For example, let's say you are unemployed. Your goal may be to find a job in thirty days. Perhaps you are starting a new business. Your goal may be to turn a profit within one year.

Create a Daily Action Plan.

The best example we can think of is our opportunity over the years to manage salespeople. We determined long ago that sales can be determined mathematically. For example, if you determine that one of every ten people you give a sales presentation to will buy your product and you need to make three sales per day, what do you do? That's right, you make thirty presentations a day. We believe strongly in creating a daily action plan to overcome your crisis. The tendency is to become depressed and actually make less effort than in normal circumstances.

After seeing us glide through a crisis, people often ask, "How do you stay so focused?"

"Don't let the little things bother you," we respond. "And the way we see it, everything is a little thing." Not getting sidetracked emotionally has made problem solving an easier task.

Monitor the Plan.

It is important to monitor your plan. In many ways it is just as important as creating it in the first place. To monitor your plan is essentially to track the progress of your actions. For most people, the best way to do this is through some form of a daily diary or log book. Monitoring both actions and results is imperative.

We have always made a commitment to meet at least once each month to review the progress of our companies. At these meetings we look at the financial statements and also review the ongoing goals of the organization. This month-by-month monitoring has been a great tool in our growth of dozens of businesses.

SIX

SEEK
COUNSEL OF
THE WISE

JUST AS Mary, the mother of Jesus, asked for His help when the wedding party ran out of wine, we must also ask for help when we need it. Mary could have avoided requesting aid by using a variety of excuses: Why ask for His help? He must already know we are out of wine. He won't want to help solve this problem.

Asking for help is sometimes difficult to do. We have in the past referred to our office phone line as a financial 911 because of the problems that constantly flow into our switchboard. We have to wonder how many people have problems and do not ask for help.

One Sunday morning our pastor shared a funny but thought-provoking story. There was a man who had heard of a flood sweeping through the countryside. He was especially concerned since he had no transportation to a safe place. He prayed, and God said that he was not to fear; he would be saved from the flood. No sooner did the man stop praying when a car drove up and the driver offered him transportation to safety.

Surprisingly, the man said, "No, thanks, God will deliver me."

By this time the rain was coming down steadily and was already flooding the first floor of his house. About an hour later a neighbor in a rowboat paddled to the second-story window and also offered help to the man.

Again the fellow said, "No, thanks, God will deliver me."

Finally, the man was perched on his chimney as the water was now over the roof of his house. A helicopter flying overhead dropped a ladder, and to the surprise of the pilot the man again refused help, insisting, "God will deliver me." Minutes later the man drowned.

As the story goes, in heaven the man asked God why he had drowned and why he was not delivered as the Lord had promised him. God responded by saying, "I sent a car, a boat and finally a helicopter, and in each case you refused My help!"

We always think of this story when we hear about people who do not accept assistance from others. For example, just this past weekend an older couple asked us to help their daughter. We asked them why she was not asking for herself.

"She has numerous problems," they said, "but

she doesn't seem to be willing to accept help."

Obviously we could not give this woman help until she was ready to ask for and receive it.

> So I say to you: Ask and it will be given to you; seek and you will find; knock and the door will be opened to you. For everyone who asks receives; he who seeks finds; and to him who knocks, the door will be opened.
>
> Which of you fathers, if your son asks for a fish, will give him a snake instead?...If you then, though you are evil, know how to give good gifts to your children, how much more will your Father in heaven give the Holy Spirit to those who ask him! (Luke 11:9-13).

This is an incredible section of Scripture to review. The most interesting observation is all the action — seek, knock, ask. The notion of sitting back and waiting for a solution is clearly eliminated here.

FIVE PLACES TO GO FOR HELP

1. God
2. Your pastor
3. Fellow church members
4. Family members
5. Friends

We really believe in the truth of Romans 8:28:

"In all things God works for the good of those who love him, who have been called according to his purpose." The major principle to be gleaned from this verse is that, regardless of how bad things are, there is a purpose for what is happening, and God will bring good from bad circumstances.

Let's say, for example, that you are in need and have never asked "anybody for anything," as the old saying goes. Because of your crisis, for the first time you ask for someone else's help. The process of overlooking your pride and asking for help may have been the character-building experience God had planned for you.

Additionally, personal crisis has produced some of the greatest ministers and counselors. Former prisoners have started prison ministries, and individuals abused as children have pioneered child abuse protection programs. Many other examples abound. We call these great ministers "empathizers." Sympathy is understanding how someone feels, while empathy is experiencing their feelings with them.

Be open-minded for the solution to your problem.

One day Peter and John were going up to the temple at the time of prayer — at three in the afternoon. Now a man crippled from birth was being carried to the temple gate called Beautiful, where he was put every day to beg from those going into the temple courts. When he saw Peter and John about to enter, he asked them for money. Peter looked straight at him, as did John. Then Peter said, "Look at us!" So the man gave them his attention, expecting to get something from them.

Then Peter said, "Silver or gold I do not have, but what I have I give you. In the name of Jesus Christ of Nazareth, walk." Taking him by the right hand, he helped him up, and instantly the man's feet and ankles became strong (Acts 3:1-7).

What is interesting here is that Peter and John did not give the man money as he requested, but rather, empowered by the Holy Spirit, they offered him healing.

Instead of meeting his short-term need of money, they met his greater need — health. Don't limit God by expecting Him to meet your financial need only through a downpour of money from heaven!

I remember a man who once came to us for counseling because he could not find a job. He described his situation as desperate and stated he had interviewed all over town and could not even get hired at a convenience store. We asked him to come to our office as if he were going to an interview — to bring a resumé and dress as he would have dressed.

To our surprise he showed up in a tattered golf shirt; his hair was long and dirty; and his resumé was difficult to read and contained numerous typographical errors. We bought the man a white dress shirt and a tie and counseled him on his appearance and presentation in an interview. Several days later he excitedly informed us he had finally landed a job! Some may have thought the solution was to give him money, but it wasn't.

FINANCIAL CPR

SIX TYPES OF HELP THAT CAN PROVIDE
THE SOLUTION TO YOUR CRISIS

1. Prayer

2. Financial gifts or loans

3. Wise counsel

4. Employment

5. Health

6. Forgiven debts

God has specifically given gifts and abilities to all Christians. One of the most wonderful of these is the gift of giving. Countless Christian brothers and sisters are poised and waiting to meet your needs, if they only knew what they were.

Don't hide your crisis. Let your needs be known. Everyone has times of need, and sharing your crisis situation can put you well on the way to a solution.

SEVEN

REMEMBER: ALL YOU CAN DO IS ENOUGH

Those who hope in the Lord will renew their strength. They will soar on wings like eagles; they will run and not grow weary, they will walk and not be faint.

Isaiah 40:31

Be still, and know that I am God.

Psalm 46:10

THERE COMES a point in our problem-solving process when we have done all that can be done — just as we glean from the biblical account of the first miracle. After we have done everything that can be done, it is time to rest our minds. Waiting on God to provide can be the most difficult step in the process. As we have been discussing in these first few chapters, the greatest battle is overcoming the emotional stress of our circumstances. Knowing when to stop, relax and release is crucial.

Please don't misunderstand the message of this chapter. We are not advocating a lazy, lackluster effort in solving your problems, but there comes a time when you need to stop and recharge your batteries.

During this period of rest many ideas will come to you, and your solution will become clearer. There is no doubt that God still speaks to us today. The only question is, Are we listening? Sadly, for many people, prayer is a one-sided activity: they talk, and God listens. But this quiet time of relaxation is the perfect opportunity to let God speak while we listen — a new exercise for most of us.

Both of us have had incredible ideas for solutions to problems while walking down the beach, driving in the car or working around the house. God may wonder why people don't take the time to stop and listen more often.

FOUR WAYS TO RELAX

1. Prayer
2. Family time
3. Exercise
4. Travel

Prayer

Many Middle-Eastern religions practice meditation and claim that it causes great mental rejuvenation. Although this chapter is not intended to be a theological discussion on meditation, we do know that prayer is a great reliever of stress. Setting a time for daily Bible reading and prayer is not just a good thing to do spiritually, but it also provides a means of resting physically and emotionally.

Prayer is not for God's benefit; it is for ours. Some people view Christianity as a list of dos and don'ts. But what many have learned through personal tragedy is that the dos and don'ts are not for God's benefit but for ours.

The greatest relief from stress comes through getting to know our Creator and understanding His will for our lives.

Family Time

Both of us are blessed with a loving spouse and two children. Family time is important to us. In times of waiting for an answer, a great stress reliever is spending time with our loved ones. Whether it's building with blocks or playing catch, children seem to know how to conquer stress (until they figure out there is an opposite sex!).

We have also learned that talking through the situation with a spouse can be great therapy. More than anything, this is not a time to lock our families out of our lives. Single people can find support from friends, parents or other family members.

Exercise

A recent cassette program we were listening to about avoiding burnout placed a great emphasis on

45

exercise. In our opinion, exercise is one of the greatest stress releasers we have experienced. Whether it is jogging, bike riding, swimming or aerobics, giving your body a physical workout provides incredible rejuvenation. For some people, just walking a few blocks can reduce their stress level significantly.

You have probably read stories about people who are fanatics about exercise. Once you experience the mental stress release that physical exercise provides, you will become a fanatic about it also. Interestingly enough, most people going through a crisis actually reduce their physical activity. This reduced physical activity creates an endless cycle of depression. Psychologists say that if you smile when you are sad, you can fool your mind into adopting a happy mood. So if you make exercise an integral part of your relaxation routine, it will soon become a pleasant habit.

Travel

How can I travel? I am having a financial crisis! It can be done — and should be. Travel is part of the therapy.

Both of us over the years have had the opportunity to do a great deal of traveling. Although at times we were tired of the "road life," there is something about changing your environment that provides a relief from stress. If you cannot afford to stay at a hotel, how about roughing it in a tent at a campground? Another option would be to visit relatives. Also, many churches offer access to wilderness retreats at low prices. The possibilities are endless, and a change of environment for a day or two can provide enormous benefits.

We recently heard a radio interview with the author of a book titled *When I Relax I Feel Guilty*. One of our employees requested a Friday afternoon off to go purchase a Christmas tree. In our memory, it was the first time he had ever taken any time off in almost a year of employment.

Friday came, and he said, "I don't feel right about this. Maybe I should stay and work and forget about a Christmas tree this year." He was feeling guilty over relaxing. We quickly applied financial CPR and made him leave to meet his family and get his Christmas tree.

> Thus the heavens and the earth were completed....
> By the seventh day God had finished the work he had been doing; so on the seventh day he rested from all his work (Gen. 2:1-2).

Just as our Creator rested when the job was done, we must also rest when our work is completed.

47

EIGHT

EXPECT A MIRACLE

MANY PEOPLE in financial crisis hope for a miracle. They spend hours of time thinking, If only [whatever it might be] would happen, my problems would be solved.

How close they are, but yet so far.

Hope is good. But hope plus belief equals faith, and faith is what delivers.

> Jesus replied, "I tell you the truth, if you have faith and do not doubt, not only can you do what was done to the fig tree, but also you can say to this mountain, 'Go, throw yourself into the sea,' and it will be

done. If you believe, you will receive whatever you ask for in prayer" (Matt. 21:21-22).

Isn't this a powerful statement for your life?

Jesus is telling you the specific answer to your problem. He even highlights it with "I tell you the truth."

If you believe (and you must truly believe it in your very soul), God will answer your prayers.

Now before you jump up and start praying for a million dollars, let's put it all in perspective. For prayer to work, your heart must be right. Anyone who would simply wish for a million dollars obviously doesn't have his heart where it ought to be, and it is doubtful the money would be forthcoming. However, if your heart is right and you believe, then your prayer will be answered. The key word here is answer.

When we think of faith and belief, we are reminded of the story of Jairus, a ruler in Jesus' time. Jairus's problem was one of the most dreaded, the greatest fear of almost every parent: His daughter was dying.

Jairus exemplified faith. He pleaded with the Master simply to come and place His hands on the child, knowing that if He did so she would live. Jesus agreed to go with him to his home. Sadly, as they approached the house, men rushed outside to break the news. Jairus was too late. His daughter was dead.

Can you imagine how Jairus felt? If only he had hurried faster. If only people had not delayed them on their trip to the house. If only Jesus hadn't stopped to heal the woman who touched His coat

(Mark 5:24-35). All of these "if onlys" might have crossed another person's mind had they found themselves in this position.

At this very moment, however, Jesus gives Jairus the answer to his crisis and ours: "Don't be afraid; just believe" (Mark 5:36).

Jairus's faith was answered. While others laughed at Jesus when He said, "The child is not dead," Jairus and his wife held firm. Then He took hold of the girl's hand and said to her, "Little girl, I say to you, get up!" (see Mark 5:39-41). The girl stood up and began walking.

Faith was rewarded.

If prayer and belief are the answer to our problems, does that mean we should sit idle when we are faced with a problem? We don't think so. Time and time again we are reminded in Scripture that we must seek solutions. We must take actions to move toward answers.

One day Jesus was teaching the people. Multitudes had come from far away to hear what He had to say and to see the healings He performed. You can imagine how crowded it must have been. To compound matters, Jesus was inside the home of a friend. It was in this crowded situation that four men arrived carrying a paralyzed man on a mat. They wanted desperately to get this man, their friend, to Jesus. They knew that if they did so, he would be healed. Unfortunately, they couldn't get through the throng of people.

It is at this point that many fail. They look at insurmountable odds and give up in despair. These men did not. Instead, they climbed up on top of the house and literally made a hole in the roof.

Can you imagine the scene below? Jesus was

speaking and healing the people around Him, when all of a sudden someone started cutting a hole in the roof. Moments later a mat was lowered so that the paralyzed man lay right before Jesus.

What did Jesus think about the actions of these men?

> When Jesus saw their faith, he said to the paralytic, "Son, your sins are forgiven....
> "Get up, take your mat and go home" (Mark 2:5,11).

From this lesson we can conclude that our actions are also an element of success. In fact, if we were to use a formula for observations, we might say that hope + belief = faith + action = results.

Now you have it — our seven-step prescription for any financial crisis. Let's review it.

Step 1: Define the Crisis.
Be specific. Realize that every problem contains the key to its own solution.

Step 2: Begin With the End in Mind.
Set goals that will solve your problem. Focus on the solution.

Step 3: Remain Calm.
Create a habit of overcoming fear.

Step 4: Develop Your Own Success Formula.
Research and gather facts.

Step 5: Seek Counsel of the Wise.
Pray and ask for guidance.

Step 6: Remember: All You Can Do Is Enough.
Release your worry to the Lord.

Step 7: Expect a Miracle.
Apply the formula of faith:

Hope + Belief = Faith + Action = Results.

Now that you know what is required of you to solve your financial problems, let's use them in very specific examples of today's most challenging financial difficulties. It is our hope that you face none of these problems. However, by practicing the CPR procedures, you will be armed to help yourself or anyone else who finds himself faced with these or other similar misfortunes. Even though you hope you will never need to use medical CPR, it is comforting to know you can if the need arises.

NINE

Working
With
Creditors

IN THE past decade the number of personal bankruptcies has doubled. Although Congress is threatening banks with putting a ceiling on credit card interest rates, many banks are still charging over 20 percent APR (annual percentage rate) on their credit cards. (See the end of this chapter for a list of low-interest-rate credit cards.)

The Bible, written thousands of years ago, offers wisdom for today's credit crisis. We learn in Proverbs 22:7 that being in debt means being a slave: "The rich rule over the poor, and the borrower is servant to the lender." We will develop this thought throughout the chapter and discuss when going into debt makes sense and when it doesn't. But it's fair for us to agree that debt can sometimes create financial bondage.

The next lesson we learn from Scripture is in Psalm 37:21: "The wicked borrow and do not repay." A Christian is not prohibited from having debt. This verse does not say it is wicked to borrow; rather the ungodly action is not paying back the funds borrowed.

Many well-meaning Christians who speak on the subject state that believers are forbidden in the Bible from entering into debt. They usually quote Romans 13:8 (KJV): "Owe no man any thing."

Unfortunately, they make exceptions to the biblical principle they create. On the one hand, they take the position that the Bible says Christians cannot go into debt. These same people exclude homes, stating that residences are so expensive that a person could never buy one by paying cash. Many then go further to say that automobiles are another exception; since they are also so expensive, they could never be paid for without some type of financing.

The problem is, once we set a biblical precedent and claim that a principle exists (in this case, a Christian cannot owe money to anyone), we cannot go back and make exceptions to that principle any more than we can for principles such as "Thou shalt not kill, thou shalt not steal or thou shalt not lie." We hope our point is so clear that there will be no misunderstanding. We are not encouraging you to go into debt, but we are simply pointing out that debt, used wisely, may in fact be a winning approach for the Christian.

A perfect example is home ownership. If the

church followed the principle that a Christian can never have debt, then many people would be forced to rent for the rest of their lives. Most would likely end up on the short end of the stick financially at retirement, without having any ownership or equity built up in a property.

The real truth in Romans 13:8 can be found by reading the entire chapter. However, for this purpose, let's just look at Romans 13:7-8 and see what meaning we can derive.

> Give everyone what you owe him: If you owe taxes, pay taxes; if revenue, then revenue; if respect, then respect; if honor, then honor.
> Let no debt remain outstanding, except the continuing debt to love one another, for he who loves his fellow-man has fulfilled the law.

It seems to be a mistake to think these verses forbid the use of credit on the part of the believer. The emphasis seems to be on honoring our commitments and also on having an inexhaustible capacity to give love.

In the light of a debt problem, let us again briefly review the seven steps to problem solving.

Step 1:
Define the Crisis.

Step 2:
Begin With the End in Mind.

FINANCIAL CPR

Step 3:
Remain Calm.

Step 4:
Develop Your Own Success Formula.

Step 5:
Seek Counsel of the Wise.

Step 6:
Remember: All You Can Do Is Enough.

Step 7:
Expect a Miracle.

STEP 1: DEFINE THE CRISIS.

The most common, personal, financial tragedy is an individual who gets behind on his debt payments. We have seen people moved to tears, and of course the newspapers record the cases of debtor suicide in the thousands.

We are not promoting a happy-go-lucky, who-cares attitude about paying back creditors, but nothing is accomplished by worrying oneself sick about getting behind on debt payments. Some people have actually worsened their situation through worry. They have been unable to work because of sickness brought on by stress, problems with their marriage or strained relations with their children.

When you are being bombarded by creditors from every direction, it is important to keep a very clear perspective as to what the crisis really is. Remember, the crisis is not that the creditors are calling you. The crisis is not even that they are threatening you. The crisis is that you are behind on your payments.

We must focus on that crisis before we can develop a solution to the problem. Without question, this particular crisis is the most difficult for people to stay focused on because there are so many distractions. Although it goes without saying, a credit crisis may in fact be combined with other crises mentioned in this book, like a job loss, a bankruptcy or a business failure.

STEP 2: BEGIN WITH THE END IN MIND.

What is it about your situation that must change? Remember, don't focus on the symptoms. To achieve a long-term victory over the crisis, you need to have a specific target. Start with the end result in mind.

In this situation it is wise to have a short-term goal and a long-term goal. For example, a short-term goal might be: Within six months I would like to be current on all my payments. A long-term goal may be: Within five years I would like to be completely debt-free.

Again, an unusual but accurate observation, in our opinion, is that people in this type of crisis refuse to set goals. Goal setting is typically associated with building and not *rebuilding*, or, in this case, repairing, a cash-flow problem. We would like for the problem to go away overnight. In most cases that's not realistic. So a reasonable goal must be set, such as catching up and being on time with your payments within a six-month period. Of course, that may prove to be impossible. Maybe it will be one year or even longer.

Not dealing with this issue of setting a goal will only cause a longer delay in the final resolution of your crisis. Many people who are behind on their payments and are being harassed by creditors simply deny that the problem exists. The typical individual who does this will ignore the problem and thus not set a goal to resolve it. But the problem only gets worse. Those who have gone through this type of crisis will certainly agree with that.

The only way to confront the problem is head-on. Sit down, add the numbers up, look at where you are and decide where you want to be in the short term and in the long term.

STEP 3: REMAIN CALM.

Although you may not realize it now, running away from your problem will only create repercussions down the road. The psalmist says, "I sought the Lord, and...he delivered me from all my fears" (Ps. 34:4).

Although this was shared in an earlier chapter, we want to refer you again to Matthew 8:27, which talks about Jesus' sleeping through the storm while the disciples panicked. How could Jesus sleep while the disciples panicked? It's a decision of where your faith will be placed. The disciples, of course, had not realized whom they were with, and they had not perfected their faith in the Lord Jesus Christ and His ability to protect them.

In eighteenth-century England, as an alternative to being sentenced to debtor's prison, individuals were given the option of bankruptcy. Imagine going to prison for not being able to pay your debts.

Then in 1841 in the United States the first major

bankruptcy laws were passed. Before this legislation, imprisonment was also commonplace here for not paying debts. Although bankruptcy will be discussed in a later chapter, we wanted to point out now that getting behind on your payments does not mean you will be thrown into prison. Nor does it mean that someone is going to come and harm you physically. Although a debt problem is an emotionally draining experience and a great source of stress, most state laws protect the borrower. We cannot see any valid reason for worrying about not being able to meet your financial obligations.

At the same time, we don't want to encourage anyone to get behind on his payments. There certainly are consequences, such as damage to your credit report or possible judgments awarded against you. Still, it is not the level of problem that many people perceive it to be. In overreacting to the crisis, some people commit suicide, get a divorce or experience other emotional tragedies.

Panicking is certainly not going to do anything except damage your situation further.

STEP 4: DEVELOP YOUR OWN SUCCESS FORMULA.

To begin with, take out a blank pad of paper and list all of the facts you know about your situation. What are the balances you owe on various accounts? How much behind are you on each account? Research your situation thoroughly.

Next, break your problems down to size. How much of this monthly debt is attached to credit cards? How much is attached to your mortgage payment, your automobile payment and other personal loans? Categorize and organize your situation. Once you have determined the total "damages" in your situation, it is time to create a plan to solve the problem. *Again, the problem is that you are behind on your payments and you want to become current.* Anything else is simply a distraction at this point.

As a specific example, let's say you have determined that you are approximately three thousand dollars behind on your payments. The first thing you must do from a legal standpoint is place a greater emphasis on your secured debts than on your unsecured debts. For example, if you don't make your mortgage payment on a timely basis for two or three months, chances are your bank will be coming soon to foreclose on your property. This will be discussed in another chapter. The point here is that the payment must be made and must be given a priority. If you don't make that payment, foreclosure may be the result.

The next priority would be any other secured loans, such as automobile loans. If you don't make your automobile loan payments, your automobile will be repossessed by the finance company holding a lien against it.

Unsecured debt such as credit cards and personal loans, although important to repay, cannot have the same priority as the secured debts you are currently dealing with.

Once you have created your priority list, the next step is to put together your work-out plan. Again, let's say that you are three thousand dollars behind on your payments. After thinking through the situation, you have determined that by taking a part-time job you can add an additional five hundred dollars per month to the family budget. So if you take five hundred and divide it into three thousand, you see that the bank payments will be current within six months. What you then must do is lay this out on paper, creating an entire plan for how you are going to repay the debts. Again, special priority is given to the secured debts over the unsecured debts.

Although you are going to favor the secured creditors over the unsecured creditors, you want to make sure you pay the unsecured creditors some small amount each month until you are caught up. In that way you demonstrate as a good faith gesture that you are attempting to become current. Once you put together your work-out plan, it is important that you send a letter to each creditor specifically outlining how you intend to pay them back. For example, to a creditor with whom you are five hundred dollars in arrears, your letter would read that you plan to make all payments current; to deal with the five-hundred-dollar deficit you plan to add an additional one hundred dollars per month over the next five months. You would be amazed to learn how many creditors will work with you if you communicate with them.

Most people, when they get behind on their payments, simply turn around and run in the other direction. Many stop answering their phones, allowing their answering machines to screen their callers. If it's a creditor, they don't answer. What about all the letters they are receiving? Well, most people ignore the letters. They are thrown into the garbage can without being read. If you choose to cut yourself off from your creditors and not respond to their attempts to work with you by telephone or mail, you are giving them no other option than to take their case to court.

Once a creditor is given no other option than to sue you to regain his funds, he may decide not to carry through on the lawsuit if he thinks it will cost him more than the amount to be collected. This is called a charge-off. Many times, after trying to collect amounts of less than one thousand dollars for a period of one year or more, the creditor will write off the amount owed as bad debt on the corporate tax return. This, of course, is no easy way out for you, since it will show up on your credit report for seven years as a charge-off. That means you weren't willing or able to pay the debt, and the creditor was not willing to spend the money to get a judgment against you in a court of law.

We won't spend much time in this chapter on the issue of lawsuits. We believe that it usually does not have to come to that. In most cases, if people would communicate with their creditors and put together a plan to get back on time, they would avoid legal repercussions from the problem. The key is communication. If an unsecured creditor gets a judgment against you for the balance owed to him, he may be able (in many states) to add the court costs and attorney's fees to that amount. The end sum can be quite hefty and certainly something to avoid.

A positive side to a judgment being awarded against you is that judgments are very difficult to collect on, especially when dealing with unsecured debt. Again, an unsecured debt is a loan agreement with no collateral. As mentioned earlier, automobile loans are collateralized loans; that is, the automobile stands as collateral. In the event that payments are not made, the automobile can be repossessed. The same is true in real estate transactions. Credit cards, personal loans and other lines of credit are typically unsecured debt.

In some cases unsecured creditors are successful in having an individual's wages garnished. But wage garnishment is very difficult to implement, and in many states it is virtually impossible.

The point of this brief discussion is to dispel much of the fear you may have about your situation and stop you from playing the "what if" game. What if I'm not able to make the payments? What if they take me to court as they are threatening to do in the collection letters? What if they get a judgment against me? What will the result of that be? Most likely, in the case of unsecured debt, the result will be nothing more than having ruined credit. Not a small price to pay, for sure, but certainly much less of a consequence than many people will worry about as an outcome.

According to the Fair Debt Collection Practices Act, collection agencies are not allowed to cross the line of harassment. Many times harassment is the key reason for the stress and emotional trauma that take place in an individual who is going through a credit crisis. Collection agencies cannot contact you before 8:00 A.M. or after 9:00 P.M. They cannot call you at work after you have notified them not to, threaten you with arrest or use any other scare tactics, or practice general harassment, such as contacting friends, relatives, neighbors or co-workers about your debt. If you feel that your rights are being violated under the Fair Debt Collection Practices Act, you may file a complaint with the Federal Trade Commission.

Federal Trade Commission
Division of Credit Practices
Sixth Street & Pennsylvania Avenue NW
Washington, D.C. 20580
(202) 326-2222

Pearl Polto, a frequent guest on our radio program and one of the nation's leading credit experts, has advised many listeners on how to deal with a harassing creditor. The best approach is to invoke the Fair Debt Collection Practices Act rule that forbids a creditor from contacting you by telephone after you have asked him (in writing) not to.

Isolating yourself is not the solution to solving your problems with your creditors. However, if you are being unreasonably harassed by a specific creditor, simply write him a letter letting him know that he is no longer allowed to contact you by telephone. If he does, he is violating federal law, and you can tell the creditor you will register a complaint with the Federal Trade Commission. It is best to send a registered letter with a return receipt requested (see address in preceding paragraph).

STEP 5: SEEK COUNSEL OF THE WISE.

In an attempt to deal with the ever-increasing problem of Christians in financial crisis, many churches have set up their own financial counseling departments. This is an excellent source of help in creating your action plan and putting together a program to get back on track with your creditors. If such a program is not available at your church, you may want to call several of the larger churches in your community. Certainly, at least one will have this type of Christian counseling service available.

The Consumer Credit Counseling Service is a popular secular organization with offices in most major cities across the country. The CCCS specializes in helping people put together plans to get back on track with their creditors.

They do have one unusual criterion for getting help from them. You must have the ability, or be able to show the ability, to get back on track with your creditors. For example, if your income is not enough to pay your current payments and you have no way to increase your income, you will not be accepted as a client (see the end of this chapter for more information about CCCS).

Some people are frustrated to hear of this policy. We think it has a positive aspect to it. Why begin a project unless it can be ended successfully? If a person's income needs to be increased to get him back on track with his creditors, step one would be to increase his income, and step two would be to create a plan with the increased income to get him back on track with his past-due payments.

In addition to using a counseling service, you may want to get counsel from a friend or relative who has personal experience with this type of situation. This could be a business owner, a banker, a certified public accountant or anyone else you can confide in who has a general working understanding of personal finance. The key here is not to be a loner. Several organizations, both Christian and secular, are available to help you in your crisis. Also, within your circle of friends, relatives and business contacts are capable and qualified individuals who would be more than happy to help you create a plan to solve your problem. The answer is to reach out and allow them to give you the necessary counsel you need to get through this difficult time.

STEP 6: REMEMBER: ALL YOU CAN DO IS ENOUGH.

Once you have put together your work-out plan, stick with your plan. Focus your energies on continuing that income flow to be able to make the plan a reality. Now is not the time to become overwhelmed with stress and worry. Now is the time to redirect the energy you have been spending on worry into making your action plan a reality. As each week goes by and you stick to your plan, you will see the mountain of debt shrink. That will certainly encourage you to continue on the path of debt reduction.

Proverbs 16:1 says, "We can make our plans, but the final outcome is in God's hands" (TLB). Here is an opportunity for us to pray and ask God to honor our efforts. Once we have created our work-out plan, we will want to remember our situation in daily prayer.

Proverbs 16:3 says, "Commit to the Lord whatever you do, and your plans will succeed."

A great verse of encouragement, Romans 5:3, teaches us how Paul dealt with his adversity. Interestingly enough, Paul rejoiced in his suffering because he knew it would build perseverance, character and hope.

There is a reason why you are going through this crisis. The reason may not be clear today, and it may not be clear for several years. But God has a plan to use this situation for good if you only let Him.

STEP 7: EXPECT A MIRACLE.

Of all the crises discussed in this book, the credit crunch probably requires the most faith. In looking at the mountain of debt they have accumulated and how far behind they are, many individuals have asked us sincerely if it's even possible for them to get out of this quagmire. For most the answer is clearly yes. But only with God's help. Don't limit God in helping you get out of your situation. He may lead an individual to give you a financial gift to help you pay off that debt. Or He may send someone who will give you an opportunity to make more money by giving you a new job or perhaps a second part-time job.

It is crucial that you balance your intellectual planning with a commitment to prayer and expectation for God to help you solve this crisis. How can your situation be more difficult for Jesus to handle than turning water into wine, feeding the five thousand with five loaves and two fishes or raising the dead? Years from now you may look back at this problem and the miraculous solution God provided. It may help you to see more clearly who God is and how powerful He is. Just as the disciples said, "Who is this man that even the waves and the sea obey him?" (see Luke 8:25). You may at some future point in your life use your victory over this problem as a source of faith and strength as new crises take place in your life.

QUESTIONS

Creditors' contacts

Question: You mention that I should contact my creditors and try to negotiate a repayment plan. What are the odds of their being willing to work with me?

Answer: The odds of getting them to work with you are probably very good. In this age of bankruptcy, the last thing a creditor wants is to lose the loan all together. We would say that the odds of their *not* wanting to work with you would be very slim. The key in this situation is continued communication with the creditor; most are willing to work with you. Anyone in debt has to remember that he has very specific protection under the various consumer laws, including the Fair Debt Collection Practices Act, which gives people some additional leverage in negotiating with their creditors.

Today, one of the biggest concerns of a private businessman is potentially having to go through a lengthy collection process. If he knows he is going to get something from a customer, even if it's over a longer period of time than originally agreed to, he is usually willing to work with that individual. This is particularly true as we are coming out of a national recession. We are seeing business-to-business collections averaging 90 to 120 days when they used to be in the 30-day range. It is not unusual for businesses to work with individuals as well.

It is important to remember that you have nothing to lose by communicating with creditors. The worst thing that can happen is that they will decline your offer and you will have to make the full payment. Your situation will be no worse than it is today. Making that phone call and trying to work with them is very important and definitely the godly thing to do under these circumstances.

Wage Garnishment

Question: I have heard stories about creditors having people's wages garnished. Can this happen to me?

Answer: It can happen to anyone. Some states are more protective in these kinds of situations. Florida, for example, has some of the nation's most protective laws about wage garnishment. But a creditor can still certainly use garnishment to collect on debts not being paid. On the other hand, garnishment is low on the totem pole of things that any creditor will do.

If your wages are being garnished, it may mean you haven't communicated with that creditor effectively. If you can show him action on your part to make payments, there is less of a chance of reaching the garnishment stage. Garnishment in and of itself is a slow process; it takes a long time to get court approval, and it's a slow process to collect.

Yes, garnishment can happen to you, but whether it does is generally determined by how the borrower handles the situation. Keep the lines of communication open with your creditors, and garnishment can be avoided in most cases. (See the resource list at the end of chapter 14 for more information about wage garnishment.)

Repairing Credit

Question: How long does it take to repair credit after an individual is delinquent in his payments?

Answer: Negative credit information will stay on your credit report for approximately seven years. Bankruptcy will stay on the report for ten years. But you have the right under federal law to insert a one-hundred-word or less response in your credit file explaining why the circumstance occurred. This would be wise for people who had a medical crisis, a job loss or some other good explanation for the delinquency. Additionally, many creditors as a part of a settlement will actually remove from your credit report the negative comments they may have filed previously. Be sure to inquire about this before you make a large payment and get caught up with your creditor.

Another thing we strongly suggest to anyone who has bad credit is to try as soon as possible to establish some good credit. In other words, if you've got three negative items on your credit report, and you establish three good credit accounts, you are at least fifty-fifty. If you don't have any good credit and you've got three negative account histories, you are 100 percent negative. So begin working on establishing good credit. Try to obtain a gas credit card or go to any local merchant you know who would report your credit to the credit bureau. Do anything you can to generate a positive credit reference to the credit bureau.

At the end of this chapter we have listed some secured credit companies and banks that will offer you a credit card with a deposit of three hundred dollars or more. These collateralized credit cards can provide you with some positive credit history to offset any negative credit history you may have developed.

Using Home Equity

Question: In what cases would you recommend use of home equity to get caught up with delinquent debts?

Answer: According to the Consumer Credit Counseling Service, approximately 40 percent of all people who use home equity or consolidation loans will not actually help themselves but rather hurt themselves. According to the statistics, 30 to 40 percent will actually use those initial lines of credit and credit cards again and have less home equity and a lot more debt at the end of the process. Assuming, however, that you can make a commitment to not getting back into debt, the use of home equity would not be a bad idea. Nonetheless, an additional legal consideration would be the risk you would then add to your home. Obviously, if you have unsecured debt and you use a secured form of debt to pay off that debt, you have now increased your risk (by posting your home as collateral). Thus, if you can't make the payments, it could cause you to lose your home.

The key word here is *caution*. If you are in a state such as Florida, which, in the case of bankruptcy, allows all of the equity in your home to remain with you after the bankruptcy, then there is greater caution for you not to use the equity in your home to pay off other debts.

The second key word is *discipline*. If you can borrow on your home and pay off the debt and then not get back into debt, that would be the best move in your case. If you are an undisciplined person and can't do that, then the answer would be not to borrow on the equity in your home.

THE CONSUMER CREDIT
COUNSELING SERVICE

In this chapter on surviving a credit crunch, we wanted to share with you a question-and-answer session we conducted with Bonnie Poe, a representative of the Consumer Credit Counseling Service. Bonnie is the local vice president of community development for the Central Florida branch of the CCCS.

Question: What is the Consumer Credit Counseling Service?

Answer: CCCS offices are local, nonprofit organizations affiliated with the National Foundation for Consumer Credit. CCCS provides education and counseling to families and individuals on personal budgeting and the wise use of credit. The CCCS offices are supported with contributions from banks, consumer finance companies, credit unions, merchants and other community services where the branch is located. CCCS is not a lending institution, a charitable organization or a government-funded program.

CCCS should not be confused with other counseling services that may charge anywhere from fifty to one hundred [dollars] or more per month for providing their services. CCCS offers all of their services, debt repayment counseling and reviewing credit at no charge or a very low charge.

Question: One criticism of CCCS we have heard from our radio show is that individuals have gone to your organization and have been declined services. Can you help us make sense of this rumor?

Answer: As you know, "help" is often defined by the person who wants the help. Any counseling agency or service provides options. Our counseling is based on setting up a workable budget that the consumers can live within. If they have come to us for credit counseling, we can go over their credit file with them so they have an understanding of what it means.

If they have come to us because they are having a problem repaying existing debts and are looking for a debt-management program, we will look at the outstanding bills and how far behind they are on their payments. We will find out what debt is secured and what isn't. We have the possibility of reducing some of the unsecured credit repayment. Along with that, many creditors have allowed us to stop or reduce interest and also eliminate late fees.

We can do quite a bit of juggling with the unsecured credit items. We can then determine a bottom line.

In our debt-management program, a consumer would need a set amount of dollars to pay all the creditors. Our national guidelines say that all accounts must be closed and all accounts handled equitably. Everyone gets his or her share of the pie that is available for those consumers to use.

Question: Are there criteria that would prohibit any specific person from being able to use your services? Let's say I have three thousand dollars per month in bills and only one thousand dollars per month in income.

Answer: That's the next step. Once you get the bottom line on how much the creditors have to receive, even with our program, it has to fit with that amount of income. If someone is two hundred or one thousand dollars short, that person has a budget problem to work with. At that point, one of two things has to happen: *They must either increase their income or decrease their expenses.* Clients are always told they can be put on the debt-management program, which requires a certain amount of money each month. If the clients don't have that amount of money, they are told they need to increase their income, possibly through a part-time job. Once they have the income to make the minimum monthly payments, they are invited back to meet with a counselor and get started on the program. This is where many consumers say they have been to CCCS and couldn't be helped. The main reason we couldn't put them on our debt-management program was because there weren't enough funds. But, given the options and the chance to change their situation, consumers can always come back and go on the program.

Question: So there is no magic cure?
Answer: No! You can't promise a creditor that a debt is going to be paid with money the consumer doesn't have.

Question: What is the biggest problem area? Do you find abuse of the credit card to be the biggest problem?
Answer: We see deeper problems than that. Usually the people who come to us are honest, hard-working people who have had an unexpected financial downfall. They may have had their hours cut, an illness or a divorce, or something else that

didn't work in their best interest financially. It shows up in the credit cards, but normally that isn't the problem. A woman came in recently, however, who had very high balances on her credit cards and had promised not to use them anymore. But she had just received a new credit card and had already used that new credit card to charge groceries. She had good intentions; but the children were hungry, and we felt certain she would use that credit card again.

Question: Another criticism we have heard about the CCCS is that it is nothing more than a collection agency for credit cards. It is trying to mask itself as a self-help organization, but secretly it is controlled and funded by the credit card companies.

Answer: That is 100 percent untrue! It's really a shame that that misconception exists. Our counselors must have three years of experience and pass a full-day exam to be certified. We are very closely scrutinized by all the communities in which we are located. Many of us are funded by the United Way.

We have the repayment program and also budget and credit counseling. Consumers will come in and work for three or four years with a counselor on behavior modification. They have no credit and are living on a cash-only basis for the first time in their adult lives. Many behavior changes take place during this period.

When the debt is totally paid, the CCCS also has a four-year recovery program. We will continue working with those consumers and help them re-establish credit and get one credit card. We will write letters to the underwriters if they are trying to obtain a mortgage. These consumers have changed their spending habits from bad to good. These people will make excellent credit risks. We will go out on a limb for them since they have proved to be responsible and dedicated to their word. There is a lot more involved than funneling the money from the consumer to the creditor. Many thousands of people have had their lives changed by being able to work with a counselor.

Question: What are the various services that CCCS has available besides the counseling service?

Answer: The services are going to vary depending on the size of the office and the acceptance of the community. All branches offer basic counseling, budgeting, money management, credit counseling and debt-management programs. Most offices have education departments that offer workshops and seminars to the general public, employer groups and school groups. Many of our offices are involved in mortgage and shelter counseling, including pre-purchase counseling as well as default counseling.

Question: What is your response to the concept of bankruptcy?

Answer: Bankruptcy is, as we say over and over, a ten-year mistake. It is a legal option, but our programs and counseling are certainly much better alternatives for most people. So many consumers are not aware of the other problems that can be caused by a bankruptcy on their credit files. No matter how often you hear about it, most consumers would rather not file bankruptcy. If we can make them aware of our services and have them sit down with a counselor, we can often help them. We can look at their current debt picture and discuss with them how bankruptcy would or would not help them.

Question: How does an individual find out how to get this counseling, and what are the expenses involved with using the services available through CCCS?

Answer: We currently have over eight hundred locations of CCCS nationwide, in Canada and in Puerto Rico. To locate the office near you, look in the phone book, or (from a touch-tone phone) call 1-800-388-CCCS (2227). You will be asked the area code for the city in which you are interested. When you enter the area code, the recording will tell you the address and phone number of every location servicing that area code.

At most of the offices there is no cost, or if there is a cost, it may only be five dollars a month to cover the cost of postage and other minor expenses. Some of the offices that don't get as much community support may charge a little more, but it is still a low-cost program wherever you may go.

There is no qualifying as far as income or status; anyone can use the service. We all work on an appointment basis, so don't just go running to your nearest CCCS. You'll have to call for an appointment because we are very busy!

CREDIT CARD SOURCES
Secured Credit Cards

American Pacific Bank
Portland, OR
(800) 879-8745

Community Bank of Parker
Parker, CO
(800) 779-8472

Dreyfus Thrift
Old Bethpage, NY
(800) 727-3348

First Consumers
Seattle, WA
(800) 876-3262

These secured credit cards are easy to get. In fact, over 90 percent of those who apply are approved. Remember, these banks do require a deposit of at least three hundred dollars, and your "credit line" will be equal to your deposit. Although you are not really getting credit, you will accomplish two things:

1. obtain a major credit card, and

2. begin producing positive information on your credit file.

LOW-INTEREST-RATE CREDIT CARDS

The rates listed below were quoted as of the printing of this book. We have listed the phone number for each bank to allow you the ability to update the list when you are ready for your card.

Bank	Interest Rate %	Annual Fee $	Grace Days
Arkansas Federal Little Rock, AR (501) 227-5654	8.00	35.00	0
Wachovia Bank Wilmington, DE (800) 241-7990	8.90	39.00	25
Oak Brook Bank Oak Brook, IL (708) 571-1050	10.40	20.00	25
Bank of New York (DE) Newark, DE (302) 451-7400	11.40	0.00	0
Union Priv/AFL-CIO Washington, DC (202) 336-5460	11.00	0.00	0
People's Bank Bridgeport, CT (800) 423-3273	11.50	25.00	25
Bank of Montana Great Falls, MT (406) 727-3100	11.75	19.00	25
Oak Brook Bank Oak Brook, IL (708) 571-1050	11.90	0.00	25
AFBA Industrial Bank Alexandria, VA (703) 549-4455	12.50	0.00	25

FINANCIAL CPR

Bank	Interest Rate %	Annual Fee $	Grace Days
Amalgamated Trust Chicago, IL (312) 822-3000	12.00	0.00	25
USAA Federal Savings Tulsa, OK (918) 664-1400	12.50	0.00	25
M&T Bank Buffalo, NY (716) 842-4200	13.25	25.00	25
Bank One Wisconsin Milwaukee, WI (414) 765-2800	13.90	25.00	25
First American McLean, VA (703) 821-7777	14.00	20.00	25
Ohio Savings Bank Cleveland, OH (800) 354-1445	14.75	25.00	25
Signet Bank Richmond, VA (804) 747-2000	14.90	18.00	25
Oak Brook Bank Oak Brook, IL (708) 571-1050	14.90	20.00	25
First National Omaha Omaha, NE (402) 341-0500	14.90	20.00	25
Mellon Bank Pittsburgh, PA (412) 234-4354	13.90	35.00	25
AmEx Optima Newark, DE (302) 454-2500	14.25	25.00	28

TEN

OVERCOMING
A JOB LOSS

ONE OF the most traumatizing events that can happen to an individual is a job loss. This is true for many reasons other than financial. Many people get their identity and self-esteem from what they do for a living.

Although no two situations are alike, many job losses involve some degree of employer dissatisfaction. Even in the case of layoffs, more "valuable" employees are retained while those who are viewed as "dispensable" are let go to cut costs. In any event, a feeling of rejection goes hand-in-hand with an involuntary job change.

If you are the one who resigned, this chapter will

still help you in your job hunt. Usually, however, a person locates a new job before resigning voluntarily, so this chapter will focus more on involuntary job loss. Let's review the seven steps.

Step 1:
Define the Crisis.

Step 2:
Begin With the End in Mind.

Step 3:
Remain Calm.

Step 4:
Develop Your Own Success Formula.

Step 5:
Seek Counsel of the Wise.

Step 6:
Remember: All You Can Do Is Enough.

Step 7:
Expect a Miracle.

STEP 1: DEFINE THE CRISIS.

You are unemployed and need to find a job.
Reread the above statement several times to yourself. This is the real problem you are facing. Don't let the other problems created by this central one become a distraction to you. Maintain a clear focus on the crisis: *You need a job.*

STEP 2: BEGIN WITH THE END IN MIND.

Remember: A goal is a dream with a date for achievement. "I really need to find a good job some-day" is not a valid goal, nor is "in the next few weeks I need some kind of work to replace my lost income." We are reminded of the Peanuts cartoon strip and how Charlie Brown handled creating specific targets. Charlie Brown would shoot an arrow at a tree and then draw the target around the arrow, always making a perfect bull's-eye. In the same way, many of us pull the trigger first and aim the gun later.

Here are two examples of valid goals for this crisis:

- Within sixty days I will find a job as an engineer with another company that is located within a forty-five-mile radius of my home. My goal is to work day hours and to make a minimum of 80 percent of my prior income.

- Within thirty days my goal is to find a job as a nurse at another hospital. I want a position that will keep me in Northern California, and I want to earn no less than my previous salary.

Do you see the point? You must have a specific goal to start working on the solution to your crisis. The more readily you can define the goal, the easier it will be to obtain.

In addition to being specific, you must make your goals realistic. As Norman Vincent Peale said,

"Shoot for the moon. Even if you miss, you will land among the stars." While you should never be afraid to set high goals, they must be realistic, or you will dismiss them as impossible. Setting unrealistic goals will not get you anywhere, so commit your goal-setting process to prayer and thought.

STEP 3: REMAIN CALM.

The worst action to take now is to drain all of your energy by panicking. One of the most important personality traits interviewers look for is confidence. If you become too emotional, you will hurt your opportunity. It is normal to be concerned, but overreacting can and does create additional problems.

A good section of Scripture to read at this time is Matthew 6. In our opinion, one of the most obvious reasons why Christians panic is because they do not understand that *God is their provider*. Their loss of a job is not the loss of their true provider.

> Therefore I tell you, do not worry about your life, what you will eat or drink; or about your body, what you will wear. Is not life more important than food, and the body more important than clothes? Look at the birds of the air; they do not sow or reap or store away in barns, and yet your heavenly Father feeds them. Are you not much more valuable than they? (Matt. 6:25-26).

STEP 4: DEVELOP YOUR OWN
SUCCESS FORMULA.

Planning is as simple as putting a goal into action. For example, a friend of ours wanted to become a stockbroker. He went to school and received his license but didn't know what to do next. Let's take a look at his goal and his plan.

Goal: To become a stockbroker and obtain an entry-level position with a firm within an hour's drive of Orlando. Earning requirements: $24,000 first-year base salary. This needs to be accomplished within thirty days.

Plan: First, he pulled out a map of the state of Florida and located Orlando. Next he drew a circle designating an hour's drive; in essence he established a territory on which to focus. Then he went to the library to review the yellow pages for every community in this territory and list the financial firms. This list numbered fifty companies. He then had his job-hunting prospects.

The next step was to create a compelling letter outlining his interest. The following is an example of a marketing letter to a company asking for an interview:

> Dear Mr. Smith: *(Always use the person's name. Dear Sir or Madam doesn't achieve positive results.)*
>
> I am very interested in discussing with you an investment sales position with your firm. I have recently completed all of the necessary course work and licensing required to represent ABC Brokerage as an investment executive.

As a manager of salespeople, I am sure you receive dozens of letters of inquiry. My family and I are committed to living here in Central Florida long-term, and my career goal is to work for a firm like ABC Brokerage. Since the age of seven, I have been involved in sales and marketing. And for the past five years I have served as a senior advertising sales representative for the *Orlando Sentinel.*

I would love to discuss any possible investment sales positions you may have available. My goal is to make a positive impact on the success of your firm and establish myself as a successful investment executive.

> Best regards,
>
> John Doe
> 123 Pleasant Street
> Orlando, FL 12345
> 407-555-1212

Don't send a resumé. Almost every expert we interviewed on this subject discouraged them as antiquated and ineffective. The major problem is that most companies receiving unsolicited resumés usually look for reasons not to hire the individual; thus, they may become a stumbling block to getting an interview.

Interviewing Skills
Over the years of managing our businesses, we have interviewed hundreds, if not thousands, of job applicants. Having the experience of being both in-

terviewer and interviewee provides us with a clear understanding of how to interview successfully.

While we could easily write volumes on the subject, we have decided to share with you some basic principles that will substantially increase your odds of being hired.

Six Rules of Successful Interviewing

Rule 1: Interviewers Like Candidates Who Look Successful.

"It doesn't matter how I look as long as I am qualified." If this is your belief, you are wrong. As interviewers, we have made immediate decisions about candidates who were dressed inappropriately for the interview. Generally, a dark suit and red tie for men and appropriate office attire for women are recommended. To be considered for the role, you must look the part.

Rule 2: Interviewers Prefer Candidates Who Are Like Them.

Many interviewing books mention the idea of mirroring, and it is an important one to understand. Mirroring is essentially mimicking the physical posture and tone of voice of the interviewer. For example, if the interviewer sits back in his or her chair and speaks softly, do the same. The theory is that people feel comfortable with others who are like them.

During the typical small talk that goes on (Where do you live? What sports are you active in? and so on), experts encourage the establishment of some commonality. For example, emphasize the fact that you grew up in the same town, graduated from the same college or participate in the same sport.

Rule 3: Interviewers Like Happy Candidates.

Some of the people we have interviewed have had such a sullen mood that it was depressing to be around them. Smile — smile — smile! And be pleasant and excited.

Rule 4: Be Prepared.

Find out as much as you can about the company in advance so you can ask intelligent questions. We have interviewed people for forty-five minutes, asking them questions about themselves, their backgrounds and so forth. Oddly enough, some of them had no questions about our company. We have often asked ourselves, Is this person really interested? By not asking questions, you appear as though you just want a paycheck and not a career.

Rule 5: Sell — sell — sell.

Both of us have been involved in some type of sales most of our lives. Early on, most salespeople learn the acronym FAB.

FAB stands for features, advantages and benefits. *Features* refer to what you bring to the relationship. Experience, education and past track record would all be features. *Advantages* relate to how these features give you an advantage over other job applicants. *Benefits* are what your prospective employer will receive for hiring you. Higher profitability, greater organization and more sales are all types of benefits.

Rule 6: Follow Up.

Another golden rule of job hunting is to follow up. Again, all the experts we interviewed agreed on this. A follow-up call, thank-you note or some other type of ongoing contact after the interview is essential.

STEP 5: SEEK COUNSEL OF THE WISE.

Among the dozens of job-hunting experts we have interviewed on our radio programs, one idea was constant — networking. The term networking means different things to different people. The type of networking we will discuss here involves making the most of your contacts. In his best-selling *How to Swim With the Sharks Without Being Eaten Alive*, Harvey Mackay places an extreme emphasis on building a Rolodex file of contacts. The concept is simple, but many fail to apply it.

Throughout our lives most of us have an opportunity to meet thousands of people. People at church or parties, business associates and clients — the list is endless. As you meet people, write down their names and phone numbers or get a business card. Once you have begun to build your network, send them Christmas or birthday cards or make an occasional phone call.

At this moment you may be thinking, That's great for the future, but what about my need to find a job today? Believe it or not, you already have a huge Rolodex file in your head with the names of relatives, friends and business contacts. Start immediately to write down names, addresses and phone numbers. Once your list is complete, either call the people on your list or send a simple letter informing them of your job search.

We are amazed to hear people say, "It's not what you know but whom you know," when they become frustrated in their job search. They are saying they don't have a chance because they are not insiders who "know someone."

They are partially right. It *is* more whom you know than what you know! The real truth, however, is that everyone knows hundreds of people. All of us are corporate insiders if we choose to be. We have heard many stories of individuals just starting to call their contacts, and even before getting through the list they had a job. The answer was always there; they just needed to take the initiative.

Another interesting method when contacting companies is to go to the library and request the Sunday newspaper from the previous six months. Call the older classified ads before calling the ads in the current edition of the newspaper. Many of the companies that had advertised may now need another employee in the same role, or perhaps the original person who was hired didn't work out. Almost no one will be calling on these companies since their advertisements appeared months earlier; hence, your competition will be minimal.

Don't Count on Job Search Agencies
According to the United States Department of Labor, most people who find jobs do not find them through job search agencies. The statistics show that 5 to 10 percent of job seekers obtain their jobs through classified advertisements in the newspaper. Another 5 to 10 percent locate them through

job search agencies. However, nearly 80 to 90 percent of all successful employment seekers find their jobs by networking.

Let us re-emphasize how important it is for you to use your existing contacts and not rely on the classified section of the newspaper or on job search agencies. People who have just lost their jobs are targets for scheme and scam artists who will try to sell them publications or lists of available jobs and even charge them to find another job through their recruiting agency. Use great caution when paying someone to help you find your next job. Whether it means paying a person who is selling you a list or a publication or someone who calls himself an executive recruiter, be careful.

According to Ken and Sheryl Dawson, authors of *Job Search: The Total System*, the most highly respected executive recruiting firms fall into a category known as the "nifty-fifty." This list of the nifty-fifty appears annually in the *Executive Recruiter News*, which is available at your local library. These top fifty recruiting firms are essentially on retainer for the nation's largest companies to find them qualified and experienced candidates for positions as they become available. Their compensation comes from the companies for which they are recruiting, not from the people they locate. That's the difference between a legitimate recruiter and one who is simply panhandling from people in a desperate situation.

Every few weeks it is interesting to watch the local news affiliates pick up on a new scam that's just been developed to hit those people who are out of work. Again, these scams range from selling lists of available jobs — which are nothing more than copies of ads out of the classified pages — to people who are charging exorbitant fees to help someone find his next job. Be very careful. Ask for references. More than likely, the best advice is not to work with anyone unless the fee is being paid by the recruiting company, which is generally the standard in today's business recruiting.

Resumés

As we mentioned earlier in this chapter, mailing off a resumé is no longer the way to begin a job search. The best approach is to send out a marketing letter outlining your interests, abilities and qualifications for a position with the prospective company. Eventually, however, the issue of a resumé will come up, and your prospective employer will ask for that resumé — most likely at the first interview, and in some cases before the first interview.

The question now is, How do I put together my resumé? There are many opinions on this subject. Some prefer the old, formal approach to writing a resumé; others recommend a new, looser format.

Putting together a resumé is easier now than it ever was since there are literally hundreds of resumé preparation services cropping up around the country. You will see them advertised in your local newspaper. People who make their living by putting together resumés week after week are certainly qualified to direct you as to the best ways to present yourself on paper.

Let us point out, however, that we can't forget number five in our rules for successful interviewing: Sell — sell — sell. The same is true for your resumé. Remember, you are selling yourself. You are the commodity, and you are the salesperson selling the commodity.

People buy benefits. Let us say that again: *People buy benefits.* No matter how you choose to draw up your resumé — whether you use an older, more formal approach or one of the newer, less formal approaches — be sure to allow plenty of space to list the benefits your last employer enjoyed as a result of your employment. Awards, sales goals and quotas you've reached, new developments, new ideas — all are accomplishments which you've achieved in the past and which you plan to continue to provide for your new employer.

A prospective employer asks, Will this person add value to my company? Will I be better off with or without him or her? If your resumé is simply a chronological listing of all the colleges you've attended and all the places you've worked, then don't use it; it will probably do you more harm than good. Your resumé should be accomplishment-oriented without being egotistical. There is a fine balance between the two.

After you have completed your resumé, show it to two or three friends who own their own businesses. They will serve as an excellent focus group to tell you whether your resumé is impressive and whether it would sell them if they were in a position to hire a person with your skills.

A book we highly recommend on the subject of resumé preparation is *You're Hired* by Asa Fisk. Of course, this goes without saying, but be sure your resumé is neat, without wrinkles or coffee stains. This is not the time to look sloppy.

STEP 6: REMEMBER: ALL YOU CAN DO IS ENOUGH.

Again, as we mentioned earlier in the chapter, the last thing you need at this point is to become overwhelmed with stress and worry about the fact that you are out of work. If you have sincerely followed the principles in this chapter, you are doing what needs to be done. If anything, stop to congratulate yourself. Maybe you should take a couple of days, as we suggested earlier, and get away from your environment, perhaps on a weekend when your job hunting will have to stop anyway.

This is not the time to beat up on yourself. We're not saying this to encourage you to make less than a full effort. But when you can reasonably conclude that you are doing enough to solve the problem, let your mind relax, and don't place yourself under the stress that is so common in circumstances of financial crisis.

STEP 7: EXPECT A MIRACLE.

Just as in the model given in the early part of this book — Jesus changing the water into wine — now is your opportunity to expect a miracle. Many people believe that if we take steps to solve our problems, we are excluding God from being involved in solving the problem. A good example of this is religions that don't believe in using doctors. Their position is that if you are sick, you should pray that God will heal you. In their opinion, going to a doctor shows a lack of faith. That is absolutely false.

In Scripture we find that taking steps to solve

our own problems is part of the process. Some people try to solve the entire problem on their own and exclude God. That is what we are asking you to avoid as we review the last point in this chapter — expect a miracle. After you have done everything you can, spend the additional time and energy in prayer and expectation for that miracle.

The saying "God helps those who help themselves" is certainly not a quote from Scripture, as many people believe, but we think it could contain a biblical principle. God wants to help you solve your financial crisis. But, at the same time, we believe He expects you to do all that can be done humanly. If you have followed the principles we have outlined, you have certainly accomplished that.

Now is the time for you to look to God to honor your efforts and help you in solving your problem. Many people discount the value of prayer. Thousands of books have probably been written on the subject of prayer. Don't miss the opportunity to ask the Lord to help you by blessing your efforts and allowing those contacts you've made and those phone calls and letters you've sent to be effective. He will if you will only ask Him.

As we close this chapter, we would like to re-emphasize that losing a job is by far one of the most devastating ordeals an individual can go through. Articles in *Psychology Today* and other publications emphasize that a job loss is one of the highest stress-causing events that can take place in an individual's life. We don't mean to seem unsympathetic to your circumstance.

But realize this: *The solution will come by focusing on the answer and not the problem.* To be consumed with the problem and spend all of your time and energy being upset is not the answer to the problem. We have outlined the answer in this chapter. If you follow the simple steps we have provided, before you know it you will soon come to the solution to your problem and find that next job.

QUESTIONS

Salary

Question: How do I determine what salary to ask for when the subject arises in a final interview?

Answer: That is a sensitive issue, and you don't want to talk yourself out of a job. At the same time you want to have some idea of the market value of your occupation. The library has a number of resources to which you can refer, such as the *Occupational Outlook Handbook*, which has salary levels for various types of positions. You also need to consider in what part of the country you live. In some areas employers pay higher salaries — for example, in California, which has a higher cost of living. And in other regions, such as the South, salaries will be adjusted to a lower level because of a lower cost of living.

We have not found a business owner who is unwilling to pay someone what he is worth, assuming that he adds value to the company. So it might be a wise idea to request a salary a little less than what you think you are worth simply to obtain the job. Then prove yourself for a year or two and negotiate a higher salary based on your accomplishments.

Another alternative would be to ask the employer or his representative what the salary range is for the job you are considering. By requesting a range, at least you know the scale they will be looking for. Then, based on your own criteria or your own background and experience for that job, you might start at the higher or lower end of the range.

Age

Question: Is there any age at which you discourage a person from changing career fields?

Answer: The answer to this is a resounding no. As technology continues to change, people must also change. Many people are learning for the first time how to use a personal computer. Many industries, such as manufacturing, are facing large numbers of layoffs. In order to get another job, workers must find another field with a potential for growth and an increase in jobs. That often requires additional skills and a retraining process.

Whether you are twenty-one or eighty-one, if you are still in the work force and you are not doing what you really like to do, or you do not see a potential in your field for long-term employment, you may want to consider being retrained.

The average American changes jobs once every five years and changes fields at least three times during his career. Retraining is a continual process. In this day and age there is very little long-term employment. It is becoming more and more rare for an employee to work twenty to twenty-five years for the same company, much less forty years, as it used to be in this country. Any employee should prepare himself for the inevitable job movement by constantly retraining. Re-evaluate your own job skills and desires regularly so that, whatever the situation, you will be prepared.

Follow-up

Question: You recommend follow-up after an interview. How much follow-up is enough, and how much is too much?

Answer: The single best way to follow up any job interview is with a thank-you note immediately after the interview. That, of course, gives the interviewer a favorable impression of you, no matter what the ultimate decision is. Experience has taught us that even though you might not get the job this time, you may find yourself sitting before this person again in the future. From experience we can also say that it is rare for an employer to receive a thank-you note from someone he has interviewed. In the thirty-odd years combined that we as employers have been interviewing people, we have received only two thank-you notes, and we hired both of the people who sent them — but not necessarily because we got the notes. There is no question that sending a thank-you note gives you a better chance of landing the job.

We generally recommend that you call once a week and perhaps send a letter every other week as a follow-up. You can usually tell by the person's tone of voice whether he is happy to hear from you or irritated that you are calling again. Obviously there is a balance. We would say that most people fail on the other extreme of never following up, or following up too lightly after an interview. Of course, you don't want to alienate yourself from a possible job situation, but again the most common mistake is not following up at all. Something as simple as a thank-you note for the interview, a follow-up letter two weeks later and two or three phone calls within a month will set you above and beyond your competition. Most people are simply not that thoughtful and that committed to following through after an interview.

Again, caution would be advised here, but certainly follow-up is crucial. Follow your own judgment in each situation. Part of our strategy during this chapter is networking, and the person who interviewed you would be a valuable addition to your Rolodex file, if he or she was impressed with you. Even if you don't get the job, it's a great contact for you to use at a future date.

Counseling

Question: Are there any organizations you recommend for counseling concerning a job loss?

Answer: Yes. Tom Geier of Practical Education Systems has developed a series of workshops and materials on retraining for a new job as well as finding a new position and the skills that are required to do so. To any interested readers of this book Tom will provide free materials explaining his organization and services. Write to Tom Geier at Practical Education Systems, P.O. Box 950697, Lake Mary, FL 32795. Be sure to mention the offer in this book to receive your free materials.

ELEVEN

SURVIVING
A DIVORCE
FINANCIALLY

WE HAVE all heard about the grim reality of divorce in the United States today. One out of every two new marriages — 50 percent — will end in divorce. This is having devastating effects on our country as the family unit continues to erode, and we are very disturbed by it. This tragedy affects our nation both economically and spiritually. Money is one of the leading issues that undermine these marriages.

Unfortunately, many Christians view divorce as just another life option. Yet Jesus said in Matthew 5:32, "But I tell you that anyone who divorces his wife, except for marital unfaithfulness, causes her to become an adulteress, and anyone who marries the divorced woman commits adultery."

We are not theologians or marriage counselors and have never been affected personally by divorce. Yet as financial counselors we are well aware of the financial side of divorce and believe it is important to address the question of how to survive a divorce financially.

In no way are we advocating divorce, but the reality is that divorces are taking place at a record pace in the Christian community, and we must learn how to deal with this issue. If you are facing this situation, we suggest you approach your church and see what counseling options are available. If you have tried everything to save your marriage and see that the relationship between you and your spouse has disintegrated, then you may need to do some things to make the best of a terrible situation.

You may also need to consider speaking to a Christian attorney who specializes in family law. Contact your church and/or local bar association for referrals.

It is not the objective of this book to discuss the pros and cons of this issue. Our efforts will focus on the financial side of divorce. How do you survive this crisis financially if it happens to you? Again, in order to do that we refer to our seven-step outline for dealing with crisis situations.

STEP 1: DEFINE THE CRISIS.

There are many aspects of divorce. The fear of failure, rejection, loneliness, concern for the welfare of your children, and a loss of identity and status are all emotions and concerns that will cloud your mind during the crisis.

While all of the issues are important from a financial standpoint, some are simply a smoke screen that will only confuse you. From a financial standpoint, the crisis is easier to define — how to survive economically now and in the future.

STEP 2: BEGIN WITH THE END IN MIND.

The divorce process is highly emotional. This is perhaps the greatest reason for having a specific goal. If you don't, you will get caught up in the emotions of the moment. Your spouse or your spouse's attorney will do something to arouse your anger, and you will lose sight of your objective. Your attorney, your friends and your relatives may be pulling at you, encouraging you to do more or get more. If they encourage you to do something that is not part of your goal, then you may be misled.

Let's consider an example. Bob and Sally Smith have been married for five years and have two small girls, ages three and one. Bob is a CPA with a good career. Sally is a homemaker. They have a small but new three-bedroom, two-bath home, two cars and a small amount of savings, which was a gift from Sally's parents. Bob has become involved with someone from his office, and the couple is facing an emotional separation and ultimately a divorce.

If we look at this situation objectively, we can see that Bob and Sally have conflicting goals. If they don't sit down and write out their specific goals, they may soon find themselves completely at odds and caught up in a legal system that promotes an adversarial relationship. When the system gets through with them, they will both have been put through the wringer and hung out to dry.

Let's think about Sally's goals. First she is concerned about the protection of the children. How can she seek a resolution that provides economic safety for them? Next, she needs to think about her own economic welfare. How is she to survive in the future? Does she have the education or training to provide financially for her family long-term?

While it would be easy to lay all of the above burdens on Bob as the "cause of the crisis," maturity would lead us to conclude that problems are rarely the fault of just one person, and practicality tells us that Bob will have his own goals to deal with.

Consequently, to have any success at solving the problem, each person will have to define his or her goals. On common points, they can agree quickly. In areas of conflict they can at least agree to go through mediation.

STEP 3: REMAIN CALM.

You have thought about and listed your goals. Now you need to pray about them and reflect on what you have set as your objectives and your motivations for those goals. If your heart is not right and your goals are misguided, your plan will fail. Consequently, this period of reflection is important.

STEP 4: DEVELOP YOUR OWN
SUCCESS FORMULA.

From a financial standpoint, a plan is essential to reaching a successful resolution to this crisis.

Before you create a plan, you must gather facts. At this point we are speaking primarily to a spouse who may have had little involvement in the family finances. The following discussion is intended as a guide to help you understand the process you will be facing. Some of the situations we discuss may sound like worst-case scenarios. However, our goal is to prepare you for whatever may happen. Your goal is not to take advantage of your spouse but to ensure that you can survive financially following the divorce.

Joint Income Tax Returns

A great place to start looking for family information is your tax return. In most cases this would have been filed jointly, so getting a copy is simple. If one is not available in the family files or from your accountant, you can write the Internal Revenue Service directly and ask for copies of previously filed returns. It will take from four to six weeks to get a response, so get started as soon as you can. To obtain this information, check your local telephone book for the phone number of the IRS office in your area.

The tax return will give you lots of information, not only about salary and other earned income, but also about the types of assets you and your spouse have. Anything that produces income will be listed, providing everything has been reported. For instance, if a dividend is listed, then you know there is underlying stock somewhere. If a deduction has been taken for an IRA contribution, you can assume there is an IRA account somewhere that has been growing. You will have some future rights to that money, even if it is listed in your spouse's name.

The tax return may also become important because of what's not listed. Like too many other Americans, your spouse may have left some income unreported or may have taken fictitious deductions. As unpleasant as this discovery may be, the knowledge may help you to reach a fair settlement with your spouse. However, if you were previously aware that your income tax returns were not honest, then you may also be liable. Discuss the matter carefully with your lawyer.

There is another reason to get copies of your tax returns directly from the IRS. As the actual divorce proceedings begin, people have been known to create new tax returns that are more favorable to them than the ones actually filed. The fake tax return is then used during divorce proceedings. Most people don't even realize this could happen and assume that the returns are correct because they are on IRS forms. Since a little correction fluid and a copy machine can change the forms completely, you should definitely compare those forms filed with the IRS against those submitted for the divorce proceedings. If you find a discrepancy, you will want to notify the divorce judge.

Bank Financial Statements
If your spouse has borrowed money from a bank or a savings and loan, a financial statement naming owed assets and current liabilities will have

been filled out. When the statement was submitted to the bank, a pledge was signed stating that the facts given were true. In most instances these statements are completed to show the most favorable financial situation possible. Consequently, by obtaining possession of the statements, you will have a signed document showing your spouse's worth.

During divorce proceedings the value of your spouse's assets may come into question; therefore you may need the document from the bank to show a fair representation of them. Spouses sometimes intentionally underreport the value of assets to improve their position in divorce settlements. For example, the judge may be told an item is worth only $50,000 when a statement to the bank states that it is worth $150,000.

This information, however, puts you in somewhat of an ethical quagmire. If the bank learns through your testimony that the assets are actually worth less than reported, the loan may be lost, and criminal charges could be filed. Hence, your spouse may be more reasonable with you in the divorce settlement if you simply agree not to disclose the information. But you may feel a moral responsibility to disclose the truth to authorities. You will need to invest much thought and prayer in this situation.

Corporate Tax Returns

A spouse who has a small corporation will also be filing corporate tax returns. Private corporations have often been used to hide assets from a spouse. If the spouse owns control of the corporate stock, it makes no difference from a practical standpoint whether the ski chateau is listed in the spouse's name or the company's name. In a divorce proceeding it could make a tremendous difference if you are aware of these assets. By knowing this information, you have a potential interest in the property even though it is technically owned by the corporation.

Corporate tax returns will be much more difficult to obtain because you will not be able to write the IRS for a copy. These records will have to be subpoenaed by your lawyer. Make efforts to obtain a copy of the returns prior to the start of divorce proceedings so that you will have time to plan how you want to react to various corporate assets.

Canceled Checks

Canceled checks may also help you identify assets you were not aware of. Many of the checks won't mean anything to you, but some may develop a pattern. For instance, if checks are written every month to a management company you don't know about, the company must be managing something. Call them up and find out what they are managing.

At this point, let us clarify that at no time do we condone illegal or dishonest methods in your search for information. But your financial survival and that of any children you may be responsible for depends on an honest disclosure of your spouse's assets, so be diligent.

Canceled checks will also show you any transfers or withdrawals made recently. Unfortunately, you may not be the only one considering a divorce, so watch for what may be conversions of money from joint accounts to an individual account or to cash. This is very common in divorce proceedings, and frequently it is the spouse controlling the checking account who is able to take all the cash out and redeposit it in an individual account. This may be unethical, but he or she has the legal right to do so. Yet you may be left cashless through a long divorce process. See the following section on "Financial Moves Before the Divorce" for ways to avoid this difficult situation.

Children's Accounts

You might not normally think to check your children's savings accounts for unusual activity, but this has been an area of abuse. A spouse may either load up a child's account with money or perhaps even open new accounts in the child's name. Once a divorce settlement takes place, the money in the child's account is transferred back to the spouse. If you aren't looking for this type of activity, it can happen very easily.

Make sure during the settlement process that your attorney obtains, through a subpoena, a record of *all* accounts controlled by your spouse. This would include children's accounts and would allow you to see the balances.

Deferred Salaries or Unpaid Bonuses

If your spouse is the primary breadwinner, his or her income will be scrutinized, and alimony and child support will be based in part on one's ability to pay. If this personal income can be lowered, personal payments will also be lowered. Two techniques to lower income temporarily are to defer some of the present salary and/or not to take bonuses. This is easy for your spouse to arrange by agreement with an employer and is particularly easy to accomplish in small companies. Once the divorce is final, the deferred salaries can be accelerated. This is an area of finance that can be brought up when the court investigates the facts of the case. But if you don't know to ask, the issue won't be pursued.

Retirement Plans

Retirement plans may be in your spouse's name or controlled by a corporation. However, in most cases you are entitled to participate.

Depending on the income level of your spouse, these plans can involve huge numbers and include IRAs, Keoghs, 401Ks, deferred benefit plan terms and deferred contribution plans. While these may not help your immediate financial situation, they will mean a great deal to you later as we talk about your own retirement program. The only point to make at this stage is that this is an important area to consider when collecting your family's financial data.

Financial Moves Before the Divorce

When your divorce comes through, you or your spouse will probably get alimony and child support if children are involved. It could be a long time from the initial separation until the final divorce decree when you actually receive or send your first check. You will need money to live on, and you will need money to pay for the divorce settlement. If your spouse controls all of the money, he or she can probably hire a better lawyer and consequently control most of the funds after the proceedings are finalized.

In order to avoid this disadvantage, it may be

necessary to plan ahead. Before disclosing an intention to divorce, make strategic moves to assure your financial stability. This may mean that you set aside some of the family money in your own name and in your own savings accounts. It may mean that you sell off some family assets and put the proceeds in your name. It may mean that you need to get a part-time job and set aside that money for your future. What it absolutely means is that you must save some money.

Caution: At this point we want to make our position very clear. We are in no way suggesting that you lie or steal money from your spouse. The money you transfer into a separate account will, and must, be accounted for in the divorce proceedings. You will have to disclose all of your assets just as your spouse will. Do not try to hide anything. Not only is such action morally wrong, it would work against you if the judge ever found out, which is usually the case. The reason you are making these financial moves is so that you (and your children) can survive during the divorce process and afford good legal representation.

Bank Accounts

Open a new bank account in your name. Use this account as much as possible to begin showing activity. It will also be helpful to you when you begin to establish your own credit after the divorce.

Open both a checking account and a savings account. Elsewhere in this program we will describe how to maximize your return on these accounts, but for now use the local bank where your family already has a relationship.

Safe-Deposit Box

For your own valuables, open a safe-deposit box. (You would be amazed to learn how things begin to disappear around the house once a divorce is announced.)

If you have a joint safe-deposit box now, remove what belongs to you and put it in your own deposit box. It is a very good idea to do an inventory of all the items you leave in the box because they may mysteriously disappear later. If at all possible, conduct the inventory with someone else present. Have him or her sign the inventory sheet with you. This inventory check can be done with a friend, but it would be even more reliable if done with a bank employee, who, of course, is impartial.

Charge Accounts

In most cases charge accounts will be listed in both names. It will be much easier to get accounts in your own name before your divorce than it will be afterward. Notice we didn't say easy; we said easier. If you do not receive an income from an employer, the credit companies will naturally assume that you cannot repay the loan.

In a sense, however, you may be self-employed. If your spouse reimburses you for performing household duties, and that money goes beyond meeting household expenses, then in practice you are self-employed and receiving wages for your work.

If you cannot describe yourself as a wage-earner, there are other creative ways to establish credit. You can ask a friend to cosign a credit form guaranteeing your ability to pay. You are taking on a real obligation when you do this, and you should make sure you honor the commitment by keeping your

111

debt paid down. Another way is to approach local stores with which you may have some personal contact and ask them to extend you credit, which you will immediately pay off. Ask them to report this good credit history to the credit bureau.

If you have a job outside the home, credit will be much easier for you to obtain because you will have a "visible means of support." Nevertheless, it will still be easier to get the credit accounts now, before the divorce, because the divorce itself will be a mark against your credit record.

You should also try to borrow some money in your own name while you are married. This is an excellent way to establish your own credit history. Borrowing money is easy to do when you don't need it. In fact, you'll find that the key to borrowing money is to make the lender think you don't need it, even if you do.

The easy way to borrow money is to use your own. Approach your lender and tell him you want to borrow money to establish a credit history. Lenders like to hear this because it tells them the borrower doesn't actually need the money. The lender will then ask you what you have for collateral. What you now offer him is a lender's favorite dream — cash. Tell the lender you will pledge to have an equal amount of cash on deposit at his bank during the term of the loan.

Notice what is happening. The lender will take your money — for example, two thousand dollars in a savings account — freeze your account so you can't spend the money until you need to repay the loan, and loan you two thousand dollars. The lender pays you 3.3 percent interest on the money you gave him and charges you 9 to 12 percent interest for borrowing it back. So you can see he just made a nice little profit on your money. If this sounds almost illegal and certainly unfair, welcome to the world of banking.

To carry this credit creation a step further, you can compound your credit through the following procedure.

Step 1: Get a two-thousand-dollar cash advance on your credit card.

Step 2: Put the two thousand dollars in your savings account.

Step 3: Borrow two thousand dollars from your bank, pledging the two thousand dollars in your savings account.

Step 4: Use the two thousand dollars you borrowed from the bank to pay off your credit card advance.

The question is, Where did the original two thousand dollars come from?

If you said "thin air," you're right. This, of course, is the reason our government has such a huge deficit, and it is a very important rule for you to remember. Borrowing becomes very easy and very expensive. The only reason you are doing it is so that if you need credit in the future for needs, not wants, it will be available. Be sure to pay off all of this money within thirty days. This will give you a high credit rating and keep your interest charges down.

Other Debt

Like most families, you will have some existing debts. Make a list of these debts and consider which ones pay for assets that you actually use. For example, your spouse's boat or business loans may have required your signature in order to get the loan originally. You would receive no benefit from these assets after the divorce (unless you get the boat!). Yet you would be responsible for the debt. If your spouse's business goes under five years from now, you don't want to go down with it just because you signed some papers that were stuck under your nose at one time.

Therefore, before a financial settlement, we recommend removing your name from these existing debts if possible. If not, then make sure you receive some benefit, monetary or otherwise, for allowing your name to remain on the loan.

Prepare for Your Own Career.

If you have not been working outside the home, you may need to prepare for a career when you are on your own.

You will need to make good first impressions, and in our society how you look makes a difference. Unfortunately, money helps. Before you launch out on your own, make sure your wardrobe has been updated for the proper business attire. If you are a woman and haven't been working outside the home, this is a major expense that needs to be accounted for.

Do the things necessary to present yourself in the most favorable light possible to all potential employers. (A weight-loss program might be helpful for both men and women.) While it would be nice to think that people are not judged on superficial looks, it is totally unrealistic and inconsistent with the real world.

Education is also an important area to work on now. Take night classes which might improve your chances in the job market. Start this process before the divorce.

STEP 5: SEEK COUNSEL OF THE WISE.

A divorce is complicated business — spiritually, financially, emotionally and legally. Most individuals are not experienced in each of these areas, and, even if they are, it is likely that emotions will cloud their thinking. Consequently, help is essential.

An important point to remember is to seek the counsel of the wise. The natural tendency is to talk to anyone who will listen. While these people may well have your best interest at heart, they carry with them their own prejudices. At this point you need sound, unemotional help from experts.

The next question that arises is, How do you find wise counsel?

This is a troublesome issue, especially as it relates to attorneys. If you know someone or have confidence in a friend who recommends one, that's great. If you don't, let us give you some ideas.

Sooner or later in this process you will be visiting the area of the courthouse that handles domestic relations. Visit it now. Not only will you get a feel for the territory, but you may also get your lead on an attorney. Talk to the courthouse staff. Be friendly and see who they think is good. More important, sit in the courtroom. Watch some attorneys actually handling cases and see if you think you would be comfortable with any of them.

Because of the time involved, this is a slow process. Nevertheless, it is an excellent way to narrow down your candidates. We think that picking an attorney you can relate to, one whom you have observed and who has excellent communication skills, will be the most important aspect of your selection.

STEP 6: REMEMBER: ALL YOU CAN DO IS ENOUGH.

The mental anguish of a divorce can leave scars for life. However, much of the anguish is self-imposed. Once you have sought and selected professionals, once you have designed your plan and begun to work it, release yourself. Forgive yourself for the trauma of second guessing and "what ifs." Put your plan into motion. Do all you can do. Then go on to step 7.

STEP 7: EXPECT A MIRACLE.

Many of us spend our lives waiting to see a miracle. Yet miracles occur around us every day. It is just that we choose to give rational reasons to these events instead of the honor they deserve.

We believe there are reasons for the trials and tribulations we experience in life. We also believe that God honors the faithful, but not always in the way and rarely in the time frame we may desire.

Remember — our time is not the same as God's time. We want things resolved today. In God's time, a lifetime is a day. Let me put this in perspective. J. W. and his wife measure the height of both of their girls on their bedroom wall. The girls enjoy marking the wall and seeing how much they have grown. If J. W. marks their height frequently, they get frustrated because they sometimes don't see any growth. If he waits for longer periods and only marks after a year has passed, they are excited about how much they have grown.

When we turn our situation over to God, we sometimes may see little achieved in a short time. But looking back over several years, we always see an expediential growth accomplished, more than we could have gained on our own.

QUESTIONS

Questions for an Attorney

Question: What are some basic questions to ask a divorce attorney before making a final decision to retain him or her?

Answer: The key here is to find an individual who is experienced in family law, as it is now called throughout the country. In most cases, if you look in the yellow pages you will find that such attorneys have designated specialties through their local bar association. They are the only people who list themselves that way in the yellow pages; other attorneys are prohibited from doing so.

Also, check with the bar association and get a referral of attorneys who have received these designations. The telephone number of your local bar association is listed with directory assistance. The attorney you hire will depend on the type of case — whether you will have a hotly contested suit or whether it is a situation in which you are looking for someone to act more as a mediator.

Mediated divorces are a growing trend in this country. They are an important development because they create a situation that is better for the overall family, especially when children are involved. Interviewing the attorney in that regard is an important aspect.

The final point in this area is a sensitive one — *fees* and *costs*. *Fees* are generally what the attorney charges per hour to work for you. In addition, some attorneys ask for large, up-front retainers just to handle a divorce case. *Costs* include any travel expenses for the attorney, hiring expert witnesses and so on. In some cases, *costs* may add substantially to your total expense. Don't feel uncomfortable asking the attorney how much the case will cost you. We recommend that you ask for a written estimate of the total expense. It is an important aspect of the divorce and the handling of the overall case.

Time Element

Question: How long does a divorce take?

Answer: The answer to that depends on the complexity of the case. If you have substantial assets, or if there are children involved, it can take a year to reach some sort of a resolution. On the other hand, if the divorce is relatively simple from an economic standpoint, or if there is agreement between the parties, then the proceedings can be carried out within a short period of time, perhaps sixty to ninety days. The true answer to that question depends on the economics of the situation more than anything else.

Legal Separation

Question: What is your opinion of a legal separation arrangement, and would this affect any of the strategies mentioned in the chapter?

Answer: We don't believe we can answer that question from a legal standpoint because separation decisions are more of a personal issue. Divorce is very serious, particularly for Christians. A separation creates another possibility of reconciliation, a time for mediation and a time for discussion with family and friends as to an alternative solution. So we don't think we could immediately advise anyone not to consider a period of separation.

On the other hand, we think it is only fair to point out that periods of separation can cause potential problems. Once a person is separated, the other individual may feel totally alienated from the marriage. This means that he or she may begin to do things that are in opposition to the other mate. This may cause hard feelings and potential economic problems, especially if that person is out creating additional liability for which the other person may have some responsibility. In other words, a long-term separation can give your spouse an opportunity to misuse the finances you share.

Based on the possibility of reconciliation, however, a time of separation should not be ruled out. If you are legally separated, we recommend that you take actions we discussed in this chapter, such as setting up your own bank account. Because separation may ultimately lead to divorce, it is wise to prepare financially for that possibility.

Divulging Information

Question: Obviously, friends and family members will ask questions about my divorce proceedings, details of the trial and any settlement arrangements that are being discussed. Do you suggest that I not share the details of the legal strategies of my divorce proceedings with anyone until they are concluded?

119

Answer: Everyone should understand that once you become involved in court proceedings, most attorneys consider it a mini-battlefield. What that means to some attorneys is that any piece of information or any action they can use is fair game. But as Christians we would encourage you to do all you can to reach an amicable settlement.

We recommend that you be very careful whom you talk to; talk only with your attorney about the legal aspects of the situation. We think it is common sense, although it may not be common knowledge, that people should keep their personal situations to themselves as much as possible and not disclose information which might be used against them in some way by another party if they are subpoenaed into court.

THE TRUTH
ABOUT
BANKRUPTCY

BANKRUPTCY IS a last resort. Those who would treat it cavalierly and sell you on going into bankruptcy as an easy answer to your financial problems are not looking after your best interests. It is an answer to some of your problems. But it is not an easy answer. It contains long-term negative consequences that can affect all aspects of your life for years to come.

Forgiven debt is not a new concept. Even the Lord's prayer refers to this issue: "Forgive us our debts, as we also have forgiven our debtors" (Matt. 6:12). Jesus shared a parable on this subject.

> Therefore, the kingdom of heaven is like a king who wanted to settle accounts with his servants. As he began the settlement, a man who owed him ten thousand talents was brought to him. Since he was not able to pay, the master ordered that he and his wife and his children and all that he had be sold to repay the debt.
>
> The servant fell on his knees before him. "Be patient with me," he begged, "and I will pay back everything." The servant's master took pity on him, canceled the debt and let him go (Matt. 18:23-27).

Although we are not advocating bankruptcy as an easy way out, it is sometimes *the only way out*. Psalm 37:21 says, "The wicked borrow and do not repay." We don't believe this verse is addressing those who can't pay back, but those who can repay but refuse to do so.

What we want to do in this chapter is give you an overview of what bankruptcy can and cannot do for you. We will walk you through the decision-making process in order to help you prepare for what may be one of the most difficult decisions of your life.

STEP 1: DEFINE THE CRISIS.

Perhaps more than in any other situation we have discussed, definition of the actual problem is extremely important in bankruptcy cases. We have known people who have declared bankruptcy for as little as fifteen hundred dollars. For that amount, a black mark was put on their credit rating for the next ten years. Had they remained calm, worked with their creditors and not been sold by the bankruptcy lobbyist, the financial blight on their credit record might have been avoided.

The first thing to understand about bankruptcy is that it is not the problem. In fact, it is really more of a solution. The problem is that you have gotten yourself into debt to the point that you feel you cannot overcome it. It is the *feeling* that is the real crisis. That is why some people go bankrupt for fifteen hundred dollars, and others go bankrupt for millions. It is that belief in the lack of ability to overcome the debt that causes the crisis. Thus, as you look to your situation you must realistically ask yourself what you are trying to solve. Is it the lack of money, or is it the pressure you are trying to eliminate? Is it the money, or is it the feeling?

If it is the money, that's one thing. Bankruptcy will eliminate the debt. If it is the feeling you are trying to escape, that's something entirely different. For while the bankruptcy process may relieve anxiety temporarily, the problems created by going bankrupt may ultimately cause feelings which are more difficult to deal with than those you now face.

STEP 2: BEGIN WITH THE END IN MIND.

Like all of the crisis situations we have discussed, you have numerous options. What are you trying to accomplish? If it is simply the elimination of debt, that goal is easily set and reached. If it is to stop your creditors from harassment, that also is a simple task. Today debtors have rights too, and one of these is to stop creditors' harassment. Knowing the rules can quickly eliminate this problem.

Is your goal simply to give yourself more time or

123

an easier payment schedule? If so, you have other options available to you including a special form of bankruptcy — Chapter 13 — that is designed specifically for that purpose.

With all of these variables, you can see why the debt process is a quagmire. Consequently, your first task is to make the decision about what you want to accomplish and then use the law wisely to help you achieve that goal.

As an example, you might write that your goal is to stop credit agencies from calling and sending threatening letters which upset your family.

If this is the case, then your solution is less drastic than bankruptcy. In fact, all that the law requires to stop a credit agency from harassing you or your family is a letter from you to them. At that point the burden shifts, and by law they can no longer contact you or your family without being subject to civil penalty.

Another goal might be for you to gain more time from various creditors or even dispute some of the claims. These goals, once formulated, will allow you to devise a plan of action to solve them.

STEP 3: REMAIN CALM.

Now is the time to take hold of your emotions. We no longer live in an age of debtor's prison, so understand from the outset that there is an end to the crisis you are facing. One of the most helpful things you can do right now is to remain calm. This will help you to think clearly about your alternatives and keep you from rushing into solutions that have long-term repercussions.

STEP 4: DEVELOP YOUR OWN SUCCESS FORMULA.

The number of people going through bankruptcy in this country has grown to epidemic proportions. The number of bankruptcies doubled in the last ten years. The only good news is that there is a lot of very helpful material available to you at modest cost.

In this stage of developing your plan you should secure from your local bookstore or library one of the many self-help books on the bankruptcy process. We would recommend that you get one from your own state since it will have specific state laws which may be more liberal than the federal law. For example, federal law allows you to exclude only 75 percent of the equity in your home from bankruptcy. Our home state of Florida allows a person to exclude 100 percent. Using this knowledge you could have a $300,000 home free and clear, discharge all of your debts and at the end of the process still own your home. We are not necessarily recommending this procedure but merely using it as an example to show you how understanding your own state's laws will help you formulate an overall plan.

As you develop your plan, one of your alternatives will be to avoid bankruptcy altogether. For example, one viable alternative is to use a counseling service. We will discuss this in the next step.

Take a careful appraisal of your assets and liabilities. If you have never done this before, it will definitely help you see the reality of your situation. Are there assets you can sell, even at a huge discount, which you can use to pay off debts? Remember, if you go through bankruptcy the court will do this anyway. You might as well face up to reality now, do it yourself and possibly avoid having to go through bankruptcy.

First sell assets which will not be exempt property in a bankruptcy. For example, you own a boat. Sell the boat and use the money to pay any federal taxes you owe. The court would sell the boat anyway and use the proceeds to pay all of your creditors. You would still owe the IRS after bankruptcy. By paying off the IRS first, you have better used your asset to pay a non-dischargeable debt.

Let us give you another example. You have two cars, both with debt. A primary car is exempt from bankruptcy sale in most states. The second car is not. Thus your best strategy is to sell the second car yourself and use the proceeds to pay off your first car. After bankruptcy is complete you will be allowed to keep the first car free and clear.

Knowing what property is exempt and what isn't is extremely important. For instance, if you had used the proceeds of your boat sale to pay off your second car since it's not exempt, the court would sell it and the proceeds would go to your creditors.

Don't take some of these ideas to mean that you can do whatever you want with your property just before bankruptcy. You can't. While people have tried to give away property to friends or relatives, expecting them to give it back later, the court will see through these transactions, and they will be voided. These transactions are *not* what we are suggesting. They are legally and morally wrong. We are, however, trying to show you that you can organize your debt between creditors, some of which will be ultimately exempt by law.

Types of Bankruptcy

There are basically three types of personal bankruptcy in the United States.

Under Chapter 7, all of your assets (except those exempt by law) will be sold to pay off creditors. Once you file Chapter 7, all of your creditors are notified. Once they are notified, they cannot contact you directly about your debt. All claims must be made to the court trustee. This is a tremendous relief to many people. After this point a creditor cannot file a lawsuit or even pursue one previously filed. He must deal with the court, through the trustee. All of your assets will be delivered to the trustee, who will sell them and pay creditors. Once this process is completed, the court will (in most cases) eliminate all other debt.

Under Chapter 13, creditors are also notified and must cease all action against you. You must work out a payment plan with your creditors which pays them all or a pro-rata amount. All the creditors must agree to the plan. This program allows you to honor your debts but gives you more time or a different payment schedule.

Before 1991, Chapter 11 did not apply to individuals. Now it does. It is different from Chapter 7 and Chapter 13 in that a trustee isn't automatically appointed. You remain in possession of your property and serve as the trustee. You are allowed to organize a debt repayment that allows you to continue your business.

As you can see, the bankruptcy alternatives are many, and you may want to seek help in determining which is best for your case.

STEP 5: SEEK COUNSEL OF THE WISE.

You can handle your own bankruptcy. But before you do, we suggest that you seek help.

There are many groups that offer debt help, including some very unscrupulous people whose "help" will only be to add to your debt. On the other hand, there are some very helpful resources that you should consider consulting before you take the final step into bankruptcy. One organization we have referred people to that has provided consistently good help is the Consumer Credit Counseling Service. This is a national nonprofit organization set up by major creditors. You can find them in the telephone yellow pages under "credit counseling."

The CCCS will assign a credit counselor to work with you. They will contact your creditors on your behalf to set up new payment schedules on your debt. They will then work with you to establish a budget to meet this schedule.

The CCCS is an excellent alternative for anyone who is considering bankruptcy. Using CCCS gives you an extremely low-cost alternative to getting professional help. A small donation is accepted to cover postage and long-distance phone calls. You now have a creditable group on your side to whom your creditors will listen. The CCCS knows how to explain to creditors in no uncertain terms that they can either work with you and recover some or perhaps all of their money, or they can force you into bankruptcy and deal with the court.

The reason that the CCCS has been such a successful alternative is that they understand both sides and are able to come up with solutions. For example, Fred has a $2,000 balance on his credit card with a minimum payment of $87.40 per month. It will take him a little over two years to pay it off. By negotiating with the store to give Fred an additional year to pay off the loan, CCCS assures that he can substantially reduce his payments. If Fred has several debts like this, he might be able to lower his debt payment by one hundred to two hundred dollars per month. This could be all the breather Fred needs to handle his debt load. Additionally, this restructuring presents a winning situation for all parties since the creditor does ultimately get paid the full amount due him.

STEP 6: REMEMBER: ALL YOU CAN DO IS ENOUGH.

At this point of your CPR process it is important to review how far you have come. You had a major financial crisis which was likely causing physical and emotional stress. Instead of letting the problem accelerate, you have taken control of the situation and moved toward resolution. Your creditors are no longer hounding you, and you are free to move on with your life. The only step remaining is for you to mentally accept where you are without the burden of guilt. It is time to move on. You have done and are doing everything possible to see that you and your creditors are treated fairly. It is now time to release the plan to God.

STEP 7: EXPECT A MIRACLE.

If you have followed the steps we outlined, you have seen a miracle. You have gone from a situation out of control to a situation in which you are back in control. *You* once again run your own life, not your creditors. We aren't suggesting that everything is problem-free. There will be financial repercussions from your former debt-burdened life. These problems, however, are all manageable. We have spoken to many people who have actually found the process to be extremely freeing because of the tremendous lessons they learned about the hazards of debt and other financial crises. They have seen the worst and have survived.

From all that we have seen and know about bankruptcy and its alternative, credit counseling, the one thing we would leave you with is a request not to wait too long before seeking professional help. This is one area in which a treatment for the problem is readily available. While the medicine may taste bad, the cure is blessed relief.

QUESTIONS

Bankruptcy Limits

Question: How many times can an individual claim bankruptcy?

Answer: There is no limit to the number of times, but as far as frequency an individual cannot claim bankruptcy more than once every six years. This question comes on the heels of a doubling of personal bankruptcies per year as compared to the same number ten years ago. As tragic as it may sound, some people are now in their second bankruptcy.

An interesting comment arose on a recent radio program when a credit expert stated that banks are now viewing individuals who have had a bankruptcy as a better risk since they now don't have the right to use bankruptcy until their six-year limitation is used up. Therefore the creditor *could* tie up the borrower in court litigation and/or garnish his wages, along with the other legal remedies available to creditors that would more than likely be eliminated by the bankruptcy process.

Effects of Bankruptcy

Question: How long will bankruptcy affect my credit report?

Answer: Ten years.

Stigma of Bankruptcy

Question: Is it true a bankruptcy will follow me for the rest of my life?

Answer: No, after ten years you can write to the credit bureau and ask it to delete that information. That's the standard answer to this question. However, there are times when you will be asked the question, Have you ever been in bankruptcy? While the Federal Fair Credit Reporting Act says that you do not have to disclose that information after the ten-year period, you will be faced with the ethical dilemma of whether or not you should answer it. Nevertheless, after ten years the bankruptcy does come off your credit report, and your life can continue.

Even though you have gone through a personal bankruptcy, as we mentioned before, you may still be able to borrow money from some lenders. We talked to a man recently who experienced a personal bankruptcy and a month later financed an automobile through a finance company that specializes in these types of loans. He paid 21 percent interest, but he got a loan. It's plain to see there is a growing market for people in these situations.

As we mentioned before, we don't feel that bankruptcy should be viewed as the end of the world. It isn't an easy answer, but neither is it financial death. For example, there is even real estate you can purchase from the government where you can assume payments rather than getting new financing. This is covered in a previous book from our organization, *Financial Bootcamp: How to Avoid America's Fifteen Consumer Land Mines* (Creation House, 1992).

State Laws on Bankruptcy

Question: You mentioned the various federal and state laws that may apply to me regarding my bankruptcy. How do I find out what my state laws are so I can take advantage of them?

Answer: Go to your local library and ask the librarian to direct you to the bankruptcy section. There you will find numerous self-help books which will give specifics as to your state. If you are unable to locate these books, the next best choice would be to call the local bankruptcy court, which is listed in the telephone book under U.S. Government. Ask them to send you the criteria on your state, which they will be happy to do.

Retaining a Bankruptcy Attorney

Question: What questions would you ask before retaining an attorney to assist you in bankruptcy proceedings? How do I know whom to use and whom to trust?

Answer: Attorneys are specializing in all areas of law today, and they list these specialties beside their name. They are approved by the local bar association and should be designated in the yellow pages of the phone directory, or you can find out which attorneys specialize in bankruptcy by calling the bar association.

Depending on the size and type of bankruptcy, you can even handle it yourself. If there aren't a lot of assets, there won't be much to save. You can buy a kit at most major bookstores, or you can use the services of a paralegal firm. If you have significant assets, such as a home which has substantial equity in it, you may be able to save this equity and avoid loss. If you have a lot of assets, it is strongly recommended that you use an attorney who specializes in bankruptcy; a licensed professional will most likely be able to save you money.

PERSONAL EXAMPLE OF
EFFECTS OF BANKRUPTCY

Because of the dramatic circumstances and emotions involved with a bankruptcy, we took the opportunity to interview an individual who had gone through a personal bankruptcy. We asked him what effects it has had on his family. For the sake of privacy, we have kept his name anonymous.

Question: What were your feelings when you first realized you may have to use personal bankruptcy because of your situation?

Answer: I felt like a failure. I had an empty and lost feeling. No one in my family had ever gone through such a thing, and I felt as though I had missed the boat somewhere. I felt like a loser. It was only by the grace of God that I found I wasn't a loser and that I could recover.

The unknown was probably my biggest fear. I wondered what would happen to me and if I would lose what possessions I had. It wasn't until I had counseled with a Christian financial counselor that I had some insight into bankruptcy. We read some Scripture passages applying to forgiven debt.

I guess Satan had put on my heart that I was the only one who had ever gone through bankruptcy. I certainly felt as though this was a shameful thing. Once I addressed the problem and discussed it with the counselor, I discovered I wasn't alone.

The circumstances were such that when I finally had the bank call on a $250,000 spec house loan, they called me and not my partners for the whole amount. I had no other choice because I didn't have the cash to pay that loan off. So my option was either to let the creditors pick what assets I had or to go into the protection of bankruptcy and at least be able to protect a couple of personal items. I found out that you don't get to retain too much, but at least it is done in an orderly fashion.

Question: What was the effect on your family?
Answer: It was very stressful. I felt as if I had failed in my business, and I also had failed my family. I put them through a tremendous hardship because of not knowing what to expect.

We interviewed two attorneys recommended by this Christian counselor and selected one. We had to pay a fee for the interview process but felt it was worth it to interview the right person to handle the legality of the bankruptcy. After selecting that attorney, we felt comfortable that at least he knew the step-by-step process. It was still an unknown for us because we had never been through it, and a person doesn't know what to expect.

The humiliating part about it was the inventory that had to be conducted by the bankruptcy court. Every item in our house had to be tallied, including our underclothes, and then they put a value on it.

In the state of Florida, you are only allowed a minimum of personal value. If someone wants to retain over and above that allowance, you have to buy it back from the court. There were some things we wanted to retain, so we had to buy them back with cash. That was hard to do since we had already paid for them once, and now we had to pay for them again. But that money did go back to the creditors who had not been paid, and they got a pro-rata share.

Question: What was your perspective after the bankruptcy? Was it as bad as you thought? Or was it less of an impact than you anticipated?

Answer: Well, I think the event itself is intimidating because you have to go before the judge in federal court, and it's almost like a line-up. There are probably fifty to sixty people per session who are there for bankruptcy purposes. The judge reviews each case and asks you questions about your assets and whether the assets you reported are correct. I think that was harder on my wife than it was on me. I have been in a courtroom before, knew what the procedures were and knew that the judge wasn't an evil man who was going to put handcuffs on me or send me to the guillotine. She was relieved when it was over.

After the court process everything is reviewed. If money is still owed for the personal property overages, they have to get that in. There is a waiting period for creditors to get together and review the assets and how they are going to be distributed. Then they have a chance to put claims against whatever the court has collected.

Looking back on it, I guess the ramifications still are not complete because the Internal Revenue Service takes a different look as far as what your taxes are. I still have to contend with that.

Question: What advice would you give to a person who is contemplating bankruptcy? If he does decide to go through that process, how should he prepare himself?

Answer: I would recommend a person not go through bankruptcy if he doesn't have to. I tried to avoid it at all costs, but, unfortunately, I had made some unwise investments and had no other choice. My recommendation for people is to work through every possible angle and with any agency that will work with them. I went to Consumer Credit Counseling. They considered my situation, but it was beyond their realm of help. But I looked at the people who were in the courtroom with me that day, and I would guess that probably many of those people could have worked through their situations. People filing bankruptcy over one or two thousand dollars don't realize the problems they will have just trying to restore their credit. They probably could have worked through some type of payment plan with the help of an agency. A lot of people are just using bankruptcy and are being sold a bill of goods by attorneys.

Question: Many people believe their lives are

over once they go through a bankruptcy. They will never be able to get a loan, buy a home or finance an automobile again. Having gone through bankruptcy, how accurate do you feel that statement is?

Answer: I disagree with that. I feel it is a lot more difficult but is certainly achievable. For example, in my personal situation, we had bought a house, but we had to find a seller who understood that we went through bankruptcy. He financed the house for us since we couldn't go through the conventional channels. We had to go out and shop for a car. I ended up not borrowing from the available lending agency, since I felt the interest rate was high. Finance companies that lend to individuals with a bankruptcy will require a little more money down and charge a higher interest rate, but it is available.

My advice would be: Don't drive the newer car; drive the older car you can pay cash for and repair the car if needed. If the body is good, you can replace the engine for a thousand dollars, and that certainly is a lot less than going out and buying a two- or three-year-old car.

I needed to learn certain things about being a good steward of God's money. But I do feel that the money can be restored. God can restore it. I certainly have all the faith in God that I can get back on my feet and do the work He has planned for me.

THIRTEEN

ENTREPRENEURS SOMETIMES FINISH LAST

JOHN WOODEN, the famous college basket-
ball coach, once said, "In order to succeed
greatly, you must be willing to fail greatly."
Nothing more typifies the American dream than
owning your own business, being self-reliant and
financially independent. That is why many of us
have had (at one time or another) the dream of
owning our own business.

On any Sunday you can pick up a copy of most
major newspapers, turn to the legal section and
find pages and pages of companies that have gone
through a bankruptcy. As a matter of fact, the
Small Business Administration states that only

one in ten businesses started will survive. The reasons businesses fail (according to the government) are twofold: 1) Undercapitalization. This means there is not enough money to adequately start the business and operate it for a period of time long enough to reach profitability. 2) Lack of industry knowledge. This means there is not enough know-how and training to properly run the business and compete in the marketplace.

Although the problems are diverse, we can still apply our seven-step process to solving most business problems. In this chapter we will also deal with the issue of a business failure — a situation that perhaps may not be remedied in extreme cases other than to close down the business. In some circumstances downsizing may be necessary.

We have both owned our own businesses over the years and have made an interesting observation: Most people who are looking at a business from the outside don't truly realize what is involved with starting, running and making a business ultimately profitable. Typically the response is not, "There is a person who has really worked hard and sacrificed for many years to be where he is today." More often the outsider views the business owner as a person who was "lucky" or born with a silver spoon in his mouth or possibly is related to a wealthy individual. We struggle with why this perception exists. If the truth be known, the perception that all business people were always successful probably finds its roots in the fact that we are not willing to admit failure publicly, although we are willing to accept praise publicly. What we mean by this is that most people who have failed in business hide their failure so well that the average person doesn't know about it. All the typical outsider sees are the successes and, thus, the misconception continues that all business people are successful and have always been successful.

To shed further light on this concept, we will share a story with you. One of us had the opportunity to get to know a member of our church who had worked as a management-level executive in a large national manufacturing firm. After many years of service he had built up a substantial six-figure sum for his retirement. He had always had the dream of owning his own business. So he decided to take this lump sum and go out and start his own enterprise. After about a year and a half, he had run out of money and the business had failed. Not only had he lost the business, but it seemed to us that he had lost his personal self-esteem. During a lengthy discussion with this man about his situation, he told the embarrassing story of his business failure. Our response amazed him, because as business owners ourselves, we could listen to his story with great empathy. We praised him for his entrepreneurial ability to relocate and his willingness to open the business and struggle down to his last penny to keep it running. We even complimented him that he had a characteristic very few people have — the willingness to risk everything to build an enterprise. His eyes lit up as he heard our response to his story. He said, "I never thought about it that way." His wife responded by saying, "I've been telling him that for the last two years."

You see, the point here is not whether we are successes or failures. The point is that when we get knocked down, we get back up again and continue to press forward to complete the race that God has called us to.

During the Great Depression, W. C. Fields, the famous comedian, lost everything he had — all of his money, his income — and found himself without a job. His primary occupation, being a stage comedian, was eliminated as vaudeville ended. In addition to these financial setbacks, W.C. Fields was now more than sixty years old, certainly well past the age to be hired for most high-paying jobs at that time. Many of us in his situation would have given up. But he did not. You see, shortly after all of these failures, W. C. Fields made the first of many movie appearances. And today we know that his legacy as one of the greatest American comedians in our history will live forever.

A book we have both read many times over the years asks what makes people either financially successful or financial failures. The story behind this book is probably more fascinating than the findings in the book itself. Andrew Carnegie commissioned Napoleon Hill to spend twenty years of his life studying wealthy individuals and individuals in poverty to find out the real difference between the "haves" and the "have nots." The result of that study was one of the best-selling business books in history — a 254-page paperback called *Think and Grow Rich.*

The chapter in this book that has been the most enlightening to both of us is chapter 9 — "Persistence — The Eighth Step Toward Riches." We are personally convinced that one of the greatest underlying reasons for business failure is giving up too soon and not trying a new idea when the old idea doesn't work. Jay Abrahams, one of the nation's leading marketing experts, says this is the very reason why most advertising never seems to pay off. Most people will run an ad and — if it doesn't seem to work — they will simply blame it on the newspaper or the product they are offering and move on to something else. You see, had they continually worked on the ad and changed it and run it over and over again with different headlines or different features in the copy, their odds of success would have increased exponentially.

Let's look at the real reasons businesses fail through the perspective of our seven-step plan for financial success.

STEP 1: DEFINE THE CRISIS.

Marketing problems.

Matthew Lesko, who has been a regular guest on our radio shows over the years, shared with us an interesting story. Many know Matthew as "Mr. Information." He has been on "Larry King Live" and a number of national radio and television broadcasts talking about how to get free assistance from the government to start or grow a business. During one of our interviews, he said something that probably affected us more than his other ideas on getting government loans and grants. Matthew pointed out that he was never successful until he came to the revelation that his entire business must revolve around marketing. He told us that everybody is involved in marketing. "If I hire a secretary," he said, "this secretary must have a marketing knowledge of my business. Rather than spending money on a fancy office and paying employees to do back-office type work, I spend all of the money that we raise at our organization for marketing — getting our name out and getting publicity." Matthew said that now his business, which is highly successful, has taught him the greatest lesson that a business owner could learn. Without marketing nothing happens.

An interesting comment we once heard at a marketing seminar was that product quality has very little to do with the success of a business. That, of course, was startling to both of us, who have always been very product conscious over the years. As Christians, we know we need to sell products that are of the highest quality, and we must be very careful to deliver not just what we represent but more than what we are representing. The speaker at this conference made this interesting observation by asking, "Where is the best place to eat in this town?" There were various responses from the audience which ranged from Italian restaurants that were famous within the city to well-known French restaurants. All these restaurants were recognized for having the best-quality food in town. He then followed up with a second question, "Where do you think the greatest volume of food sales takes place?" Everyone paused, and then of course all of the fast-food restaurant chains were mentioned.

By using that comparison, he taught us all a very valuable lesson. Even though some of these family-owned restaurants with excellent food were out there, and people knew about them, clearly the fast-food chains had surpassed them in marketing. Although their food quality was lower, the mere fact that they had created a better marketing plan gave them the success that they strived for.

The biggest mistake you can make in your small business is to discount the importance of marketing. Unfortunately, most people spend the majority of their time on product development. Although they may have a great product, it may never get sold to the first customer without a good marketing plan.

Get-rich-quick mentality.

The second reason why many people don't succeed in business is because of a get-rich-quick mentality. Think about this for a moment: Suppose you are leafing through the classified section of the Sunday newspaper and see an ad that reads, "Wanted — Manager. Must work seventy hours per week. No pay for three to five years. Great upside potential." Would that be the type of ad you would respond to for your next job? Of course not, you say. But that is, for many people, the reality of owning their own businesses. Many new businesses do not show a profit for the first three to five years. Yes, there are exceptions to that rule, and there are reasons for it as well. We can improve those figures by taking some early steps in preparation and planning and having good marketing. Still, the point must be made that if you are going into a business looking for quick results and immediate profit, you are misleading yourself. We have never found a business that has been able to provide such results in such a short period of time. Now, yes, those people selling you on starting a business, whether they represent a franchise or a multilevel marketing opportunity, will certainly persuade you that with very little (if any) effort you will be able to achieve great wealth in a very short period of time.

What does the Bible say about this prospect? Proverbs 28:20 (TLB) says, "The man who wants to get rich quick will quickly fail."

Undercapitalization.

As we mentioned previously, not having enough money to start and operate your small business for a period of time necessary to reach profitability can be the kiss of death. Again, another misconception by non-business owners is how easy it is to start and fund a business. You can believe us — it is a literal shock once you start a business and begin to realize all of the expenses, including payroll, phone bills, heating and cooling costs, rental of property, payments to worker's compensation funds, social security taxes, health insurance. The list is seemingly endless.

Please don't misinterpret our comments in this section as discouragement to starting a business or being in business, because we are both entrepreneurs and would encourage everyone at some point to start his or her own business.

The point to be gleaned here is that having enough money is one of the essential elements in being successful in business. If you are starting a home business, you may be able to launch that type of endeavor on a shoestring budget and slowly grow it into a large, successful enterprise. Again, it is imperative, no matter what type or size of business you plan to start, that you take proper steps to prepare for the financial need of that business until it reaches profitability.

STEP 2: BEGIN WITH THE END IN MIND.

Just as individuals must have goals, businesses must set good, realistic goals of profitability. We recommend being conservative with business goals because many excited new business owners will overstate the possibilities of income in the early years of the business.

These business goals need to have the two essential ingredients of all proper goal setting. A goal, remember, is a dream with a date for achievement. Your goal must be specific, and it must have a time line. For example, you would like your new business to have gross sales of twenty thousand dollars per month by its twelfth month in existence. Other types of goals would be a certain number of new customers, new prospects, referrals or repeat customers. All of these components can play their part in a realistic and meaningful business plan.

STEP 3: REMAIN CALM.

This is truly an example of a situation in which you must keep your cool. You are the captain of the ship, the ship is your business, and since the waters are turbulent and the winds are blowing, now more than ever you must have a cool head and a steady hand. One business owner we counseled was constantly being harassed by his creditors. Because of the harassment, he was not able to get any work done. Thus the business got into worse and worse trouble over the months of his crisis. The solution we recommended to him was to delegate calls from creditors to one of his top-level managers and to insulate himself from the day-to-day distractions and stress created from those phone calls. Again, we were not suggesting that this individual should not pay back his creditors; conversely, his ability to work was a key component in being able to pay back those creditors. Thus, this strategy presented a win-win situation for both his business and his creditors.

One of the premier business writers of the last decade is Ken Blanchard. His latest book, *The One-Minute Manager Meets the Monkey*, will be a classic business best-seller for many years to come. He suggests another approach to relieve stress on a business owner — delegating. Most top-level managers have forgotten how to delegate; or, more accurately stated, most employees will not let managers delegate work to them. Many managers are simply viewed as a dumping ground for problems; thus employees can simply knock on their manager's door throughout the day and bring problems to him/her. Blanchard refers to these problems as "monkeys."

Each time one of your employees comes to you with a problem, or "monkey," your goal is to help that person solve the problem and handle the monkey. The goal, of course, is to keep as many monkeys off your back as possible. The ability to delegate, especially during a crisis situation, is the key to stilling the storm.

STEP 4: DEVELOP YOUR OWN
SUCCESS FORMULA.

Business planning has been the subject of a number of books and software programs. But we have found that many individuals in a business crisis will not make a plan to get out of that crisis. They have a plan to start the business, but when things change, they're not willing or able to modify the plan to help them solve the crisis. This is very similar to what we discussed in the chapter on dealing with a credit crisis. Back to our journalism example, a business plan answers the question "How?" Obviously a business goal answers the question "What?" You must sit down in a quiet place and, in prayer and careful thought, list all of the ideas you have on how you are going to reach your goals. These ideas might include increasing your sales force, trying a new advertising campaign, doing a direct-mail piece, purchasing a bigger sign for the front of your business, having a sale or possibly reducing the number of employees. Just as we have mentioned in other materials, goals are worthless without a plan to implement them.

STEP 5: SEEK COUNSEL OF THE WISE.

There are a number of individuals who hold themselves out to the public as "business consultants." We aren't quite sure what that means, but we have found over the years that the best advice can be received from people who have actually owned their own businesses. Many times people you already know can provide the solutions to your business crisis. Perhaps these are people you attend church with. They might be relatives, friends or neighbors. Seek out people in your social circle who are business owners, those who can provide you with some necessary advice at this difficult time. Remember, one of the biggest mistakes you can make is not to accept help. God may very well choose to meet your needs through another individual, so don't be closed to accepting help from others. Over the years we have both not only accepted help from others but actually sought out that help. Free advice is available from the Small Business Administration. See appendix A.

STEP 6: REMEMBER: ALL YOU CAN DO IS ENOUGH.

Once you have defined the crisis, established some good goals for your business, created the game plan and involved others in helping you solve the crisis, you have done enough. Now stop, reflect on what you have accomplished and give yourself a mental and physical break. This time of rest will provide even more answers for your possible solution as your mind becomes cleared of the day-to-day pressures. Especially for business owners, it is often recommended to get out of the environment. This might mean to set up for yourself a home office and work there a few days a week to reduce your stress level. It is important at this time for you to become satisfied with the efforts you have put forth. Assuming that you have followed all the steps in this chapter, you will have a good game plan, and it should be starting to show positive results shortly. Please don't misinterpret the previous statements as an excuse for being lazy. That's not what we are saying at all. We are, however, encouraging you to give yourself a mental break just as everyone needs — especially the small business owner in crisis.

STEP 7: EXPECT A MIRACLE.

Think back to the time when you started this business and why you decided to start it. Did the Lord direct you to start the company? If you truly believe that He did, then you also need to believe that He will deliver you from the current crisis. It is so tempting to alienate God and our relationship with Him from our day-to-day business activities. After all, what does a relationship with God have to do with running a business? Let us assure you that the most successful business people we have known have placed God as a number-one priority in their lives. Ask your church, family, friends and relatives to pray for you and your business. Spend time personally in prayer and devotion seeking the Lord's guidance and expecting Him to deliver you and your business from this financial crisis.

The locations and phone numbers for the Small Business Administration offices throughout the nation are listed in the appendix. They can provide you with valuable free counseling during and after your crisis. (For general information, their national hotline number is 1-800-U-ASK-SBA.)

QUESTIONS

Dealing With Vendors

Question: How willing are creditors to work with a business in a work-out plan?

Answer: As we mentioned previously, many vendors are now dealing with the reality that companies can no longer pay on time. Accounts that are ninety days old and even older are commonplace. It is a standard question in the marketplace whether a business wants to continue to operate in this economic climate or close down operations. Being accommodating in terms may make the difference between a business that gets a new customer and retains that customer and a business that doesn't.

That's not to say that all vendors are willing to work with people. Some take the very harsh position that all bills must be paid on time or they don't want the account. These vendors are less likely to make it through difficult economic times than those who are willing to be more accommodating.

In our own businesses over the past twenty years, through good times and bad, no one has ever asked for a credit extension without our granting it. On the other side of the coin, we have needed additional time to pay some of our vendors, and they have all extended that extra time to us. The key here is open dialogue. If the vendor thinks you are trying to beat him out of the payment, you will have a hostile vendor to deal with. But if he believes you are in a temporary squeeze and are trying to make the payment, he should by all means work with you. If he doesn't, you'll still have an extension of time because there is nothing he can do to force you to make the payments more quickly.

Closing a Business

Question: When do you decide to close a business? Is there a formula for making that decision?

Answer: The time to close a business would be when the financial pressures are too great to continue operating it. The inability to meet your payroll and basic overhead expenses is the threshold of going out of business. Before that, there are some other signs you will want to look for, such as the current performance of the business. If you have a company that has not done well for two years, and all of a sudden it is starting to do well, you may want to keep operating. It is a personal decision you need to pray about and discuss with your family. For many people, their business is their dream — not just an enterprise they have started. Closing down their business is comparable to closing a chapter in their lives. It would be a mistake, however, to carry a business indefinitely if that business is not showing *some marked progress*.

Business Bankruptcy

Question: How is a business bankruptcy different from a personal bankruptcy? What are the ramifications of an "S" corporation form of ownership versus a "C" corporation form of ownership in a bankruptcy of a business?*

Answer: From a personal liability standpoint, there is no difference in terms of the effect on the shareholder between the "S" and the "C." In both instances the assets of the individual shareholder cannot be attacked. A sole proprietorship puts all the assets on the line should there be a loss in the business. By taking the time, expense and hassle of setting up a corporation, you minimize your downside. You seal your potential loss to the assets of the business. From a liability standpoint, we recommend that most people incorporate.

---

*   Chapter "S" is the simplest form of incorporation, while Chapter "C" is used for larger companies with many shareholders.

Selling vs. Bankruptcy

Question: Is it possible or recommended to sell a troubled business versus using bankruptcy and closing down the operation?

Answer: Yes, it is possible to do that. The business may very well have some assets that the potential buyer could purchase. An example of this would be a large mailing list of potential clients the business has dealt with in the past; they could be used as references in the future. There may be other assets that could be broken off from the business and sold separately rather than closing the doors. Take an inventory of the assets and see what may have value to someone else. Many times it may be good to approach your competitors about buying your company. Business people who have the capital to continue operating the business may see a potential in merging the two businesses. Selling a troubled business may be a preferable alternative and could put you in a better position to pay your creditors. You would also have peace of mind knowing that your customers would continue to be serviced by someone with whom you feel comfortable.

FOURTEEN

DEALING WITH A FORECLOSURE

"IT HURTS in the pit of your stomach." That's the way we've had friends explain the feeling they get when the notice comes in the mail that they are about to lose their home.

"It's an attack on you, your family and everything you stand for," they've said. "It is your whole world turning upside down."

There is probably no way to appreciate these words without going through the experience. In some of the crisis situations we have discussed, the effect is on the individual. Loss of home affects the entire family and in many different ways. Not only does it create the trauma of moving, but there are also the personal losses of leaving friends, changing life-styles, feelings of embarrassment, failure and more. Interestingly, all of these feelings are self-generated and can be altered by changing your attitude toward the experience. Yes, you may be losing your home, and it may be inconvenient, but how you handle the event and its possible permanent effects are totally up to you and your attitude.

STEP 1: DEFINE THE CRISIS.

The immediate problem is shelter. Since shelter is one of the essential elements of life, this problem will now be one of your top priorities. While the loss of a home may very well create a host of sub-problems such as damage to your credit rating, the sub-problems should be relegated to a lower priority, and you should try not to dwell on their outcome or potential effects. The people who let the magnitude of multiple crises bog them down won't take action on any of the problems. The correct approach is to prioritize your problems and deal with the most immediate and serious: *You need shelter.*

STEP 2: BEGIN WITH THE END IN MIND.

Your goal is to obtain shelter. This can be accomplished in a variety of ways depending on the circumstances. The solution can be as simple as making a back payment and remaining where you are, or as complicated as foreclosure, resulting in the loss of your home plus a personal judgment for non-satisfaction of your mortgage.

Let's assume for a moment that you have received an eviction notice. We will also assume that you know why — you didn't pay your rent. If you now have the money, that's one thing. If you don't, then your goal must either be to find a way to raise the money or locate a place you can move to. Again, everything else is secondary.

STEP 3: REMAIN CALM.

Before you leap to creating a plan, remember to remain calm. Panic is the natural feeling. Nothing, however, will be gained from that emotion, so stilling the rage and emotional pain is important. It will allow you to think clearly and be able to call upon the reserves of your strength and resources.

STEP 4: DEVELOP YOUR OWN SUCCESS FORMULA.

Eviction
Your landlord is trying to evict you. What should you do? First you should understand that a tenant has rights too. If you are being treated unfairly by a landlord, there are a host of laws on your side. In fact, in most states the laws have changed in recent years to offer more protection to tenants whose landlords try to take advantage of them. In some states, such as New York, it has become extremely difficult to evict a tenant.

Assuming you are in the right and your landlord is wrongly trying to evict you, there are steps you should take immediately. Visit one of the largest local bookstores in your area or your local public library. Ask for the section regarding legal books on your state. In that section you will find self-help

156

books about landlord and tenant rights.

The first thing you will discover is that there are a lot of laws that protect the tenant. Here are some examples:

> Civil Rights Act of 1968, 1982, 1988 and Amendments
> State Non-Discrimination Laws
> State Landlord and Tenant Act (all states)
> Security Deposit Requirements
> Mobile Home Acts
> Disabilities Act
> HUD Rules and Regulations
> County and City Zoning
> County Health Laws
> State Housing Codes

This list gives you an idea. While the self-help books are a little boring, they get a lot more interesting once you discover you have rights.

In addition to the federal and state laws, you also have the rights provided for you under your lease. Unfortunately, in many cases you will find that the lease has been written to favor the landlord. However, that's not always the case, so be sure to read the lease to see if any of it will benefit you. Even if the lease says something which favors the landlord, don't assume a court will uphold it. Courts frequently side with tenants. A good example of this is in the area of property condition. In recent years the laws in this area have been drastically rewritten. They have placed new obligations on landlords to protect their tenants. This law is called *Implied Warranty of Habitability* and has been accepted in over forty states. Under this law, when a dwelling is given to a tenant, it automatically conveys a warranty by the landlord that the premises are in safe and habitable conditions and will remain that way throughout the term of the lease. If the property falls in such disrepair that it is no longer safe and habitable, the landlord will be liable to the tenant for rent paid plus any damages the tenant might suffer.

Another set of laws which most tenants are unaware of are called *retaliatory conduct*. Essentially, the law prohibits landlords from retaliating against a tenant for something done or not done. For example, Florida law (FS 83.64) says that a landlord must not discriminatorily do any of the following acts in retaliation against a tenant:

    a. raise rent

    b. reduce services

    c. threaten court action

Please understand that the key is *discriminatorily*. The landlord can raise rents for everyone, but he cannot, as an example, single you out because you have talked to a health inspector about code violations.

On top of all of these legal goodies, a tenant will have a host of local city and county codes and ordinances that can be used in his defense against a landlord.

Once you have read your landlord/tenant book, you will be armed with numerous protective devices. Knowledge is a powerful ally, and sometimes simply conveying this information will be enough to get your landlord to back off. If not, you have another major ally — *small claims court*.

Before we specifically discuss the court system, it is important to address the biblical question of Christians taking Christians to court. As attorneys, businessmen and Christians, we have faced all aspects of this question. We believe that when dealing with another Christian, you are obligated to go individually to that person first to see if a resolution is available. If not, then you should take another Christian with you or seek Christian mediation as a possible solution. If none of these attempts is successful, then you are free to treat the opposing individual as a non-believer and go to court (Matt. 18:15-17). Your obligation now turns to your family and yourself, and justice must be served.

Having voiced our editorial view, we will now proceed to discuss one of the most underused but effective allies of the common man — small claims court. This court is a special division set up for smaller disputes (normally under five thousand dollars). It is much less formal than the regular court system, and most people represent themselves. Going to small claims court is actually very easy. You look up the telephone number in your directory, get the address and visit the office. The personnel will give you the specific forms you need to fill out to bring a court action. These forms are not complicated, and the staff will generally answer your questions about completing them. They can't do it for you, but they will assist you.

Sometimes bringing a small claims action is all that is needed to change the attitude of a landlord. He now realizes that you are serious about your protection and that you aren't going to be pushed around. He also realizes that eviction will take time, effort and maybe money — all three of which most landlords don't easily part with.

Assuming you win your court case, your eviction will be stayed. However, even if you lose you can appeal the decision, and the process continues.

Foreclosure

Without minimizing the severity of eviction, foreclosure has more frightening consequences to most people. In a foreclosure action, you will not only be forced to leave your home, you will in all likelihood lose the equity you have built up in it, possibly be liable for additional monetary damage, sustain a negative impact on your credit rating and thus influence your future ability to buy another home.

We have said it before, and we'll say it again: It's all in your attitude. We have seen people devastated by foreclosure, causing a strain on their marriages and jobs. On the other hand, we have known people who handled the process as an unfortunate event and soon moved to better surroundings. It truly lies in your attitude and your plan.

The first thing to understand is that while the notice you get contains all kinds of frightening language, nothing is going to happen tomorrow. In fact, if truth be known, most foreclosures take at least six months from your first late payment and can be fought for a year or more.

The first thing you must decide is, what do you want? Can you make the payment soon? If so, let the lender know and the problem will go away. You see, unlike the movies with Simon Legree lenders, the last thing a modern-day banker wants to do is take your property. Don't get us wrong; he will do it. But if you can give him any realistic hope that you will pay him his money now or in the future, he'll go for it.

Let us explain. Banks are heavily regulated, and government regulators interpret foreclosed property as a bad loan. If a bank gets too many bad loans on their books, it affects their dealings with the regulators and the reserve requirements of the bank. In addition, most home mortgages are now packaged with a group of other mortgages and sold in the secondary market to investors. That means the real owner of your mortgage is usually some institution in a far-off state, not the local bank where you first borrowed the money.

Can you imagine a big institution's foreclosing on your property; fixing it up for resale; managing it while it's on the market; worrying about the danger involved while it owns it; negotiating a sale long distance; and paying lawyers, title companies, rental agents and everyone else who now gets involved with this mess? Do you think they would rather do all of that or work with you while you're making partial payments or even no payments for some time? Obviously they would rather work with you.

Unfortunately, most home owners don't know about all of this or don't stop to consider the ramifications. Instead, the lender is the last to know what is going on in the family and in many cases is avoided or ignored when contacted.

It is hoped that this long narration leads you to the conclusion that the first step of your plan is to contact the lender and try to open up a dialogue.

161

Explain your circumstances, what you are doing about them and what you can do for the lender. Ask about restructuring your payments or even setting a moratorium on your payments. Remember, as a Christian, you are responsible for your debts. You want the lender to know that you are aware of that. Try to convey your sincere hope of working out a solution to the problem.

We cannot tell you that a lender will always work with you in the way you want. After all, you do owe him money. However, we can tell you that people who follow this approach are amazed at the extra time they are given and the ultimate results. If, after trying this approach and dealing with the lender, you are unable to reach a solution, then you may look to more difficult alternatives. One is *bankruptcy* (see chapter 12) and the other is a *deed-in-lieu of foreclosure*.

The deed-in-lieu of foreclosure is a process whereby you, the owner, agree to give the lender a quit-claim deed to your property without his having to go through the expensive and time-consuming process of foreclosure. In exchange, you ask for a reasonable time to move and a general release of personal liability for repaying any deficit if the property doesn't ultimately pay back the lender. With a deed-in-lieu, you will lose your property, but you will gain some time, the process will not be as hostile, and the ultimate effect against your credit rating may not be as bad as a full foreclosure and deficiency judgment.

STEP 5: SEEK COUNSEL OF THE WISE.

There are a lot of people who have been where

you are now. Look to them for counsel. Your church will likely have attorneys, bankers and real estate agents who could all offer you assistance. You might also want to contact the local bar association for reading material. In addition, in appendix B we have provided a list of information sources for issues that sometimes arise when a foreclosure is threatening.

Remember, in this particular crisis it is especially relevant to go directly to the opposing party. Seek out the landlord or even the actual owner of the property. Share your true feelings and help him understand that you are a responsible person in a difficult situation. Call the lender, or better yet, see him personally if possible. If you are serious about your problem, your lender will be serious about you.

STEP 6: REMEMBER: ALL YOU CAN DO IS ENOUGH.

Remember your attitude. In these cases there are many things you can do to be productive in finding a solution to your problem. This is good because you will have less opportunity to feel that events are taking control away from you. Develop your plan and follow it.

STEP 7: EXPECT A MIRACLE.

We believe in the law. Making it work, however, requires equal parties doing their best to achieve mutual satisfaction. You must do your part. You must be honorable to your debt, and you must not abuse the process simply to gain advantage over another, including your landlord or your lender. If you have done what you can and your heart is right, you can expect a miracle. What form it will arrive in, however, is unknown. Always remember that it may be God's will that you leave the place you are in. There may be other opportunities or other things that God has in store for you which require your presence elsewhere. Never be afraid to face the truth that what appears to be a loss may ultimately be a victory.

QUESTIONS

Grace Period

Question: How many months will a bank allow you to get behind on your mortgage payment before instituting a foreclosure process?

Answer: There is no set number of months. It could go as long as a year, but it will probably be closer to four to six months. The important point is what the bank believes is happening in your particular situation. This goes back to our previous discussion on how to treat your creditors and the value of communication.

If you have had a dialogue with the bank from the beginning of your troubled times, they will be apprised of the situation and know it is only temporary. They will more than likely be flexible with you.

If there is no communication on your part, and they are simply sending you collection notices and foreclosure notices, then the process will probably take about six months. It is crucial to keep the lines of communication open — the more communication, the better. In most cases, more time was given before foreclosure because a relationship was established between the borrower and lender through communication. That is a theme of this book — to communicate with your creditors when you get behind on payments. In foreclosure, a lack of communication could accelerate the process.

Recourse to the State

Question: Where can I call in my state to determine my rights in a foreclosure or eviction?

Answer: The best source for that type of information is your local library. You will find reference self-help books under your particular state which will give you the landlord/tenant act laws.

Retaining an Attorney

Question: Is it necessary in a foreclosure to retain an attorney? If so, when is the proper time?

Answer: This answer would be based on when you thought you were going to lose the property. If you felt you could accumulate the money in a short period of time and pay the bank, we don't think it would be necessary to retain an attorney. If you think you cannot come up with the money and that you might eventually lose the property, then the assistance of an attorney would be necessary. The attorney will ultimately help you obtain more time.

If you have a large amount of equity in the property, the risk of losing it is certainly worth hiring a professional. Anytime you have someone acting as a third party buffer, your chances in a negotiation are better.

If your equity is small, you must look at the particular laws of your state to determine if you have a potential for a *deficiency judgment*. A deficiency judgment means that the bank or lender would be able to attach your personal assets should the mortgage not be paid at the actual foreclosure sale. If there is a potential of a deficiency judgment and you have other assets that the lender could attach, then it is very important to have a negotiator to assist you since he or she may be able to negotiate with the bank to release you from that additional liability. This is commonly done with banks to avoid a lengthy and very expensive process of foreclosure.

Effects of Foreclosure

Question: If I lose my home to foreclosure, can I ever be a home owner again?

Answer: Absolutely! We have discovered numerous facts about buying property even without credit. We have mentioned some of these in this book, as well as in *Financial Boot Camp* (Creation House, 1992) and *The American Dream* (see the Financial Boot Camp order list in the back of this book).

You could assume a government loan. Or you might find a motivated seller who could allow you to assume a VA or FHA mortgage with no qualifying conditions. There are also many people who will provide you financing for some part, if not all, of the transaction. Finally, there are those who offer third-party types of loans. These people advertise that they have money to loan against real estate. They are looking for a higher return on their money than they can get in a CD and will probably charge you a higher interest rate because of the higher risk perceived in lending to someone with your credit history.

To close the book on ever being able to purchase another home because you have lost one is certainly an overreaction. The foreclosure will stay on your credit report for seven years, but a number of unconventional sources of money still exist for buying another home.

FIFTEEN

THE GAME AIN'T OVER TILL IT'S OVER

A NEW PERSPECTIVE

O ften when we face a trial we can be affected dramatically because of our perspective. This book has addressed everything from bankruptcy to divorce. We could think of no better way to end than to help you create a new perspective — an eternal perspective.

If you *knew* that you would win the game, would any mid-game setbacks cause you to worry? Yet that is what the Lord promises in John 14:1-3:

Do not let your hearts be troubled. Trust

168

in God; trust also in me. In my Father's house are many rooms; if it were not so, I would have told you. I am going there to prepare a place for you. And if I go and prepare a place for you, I will come back and take you to be with me that you also may be where I am.

THE PURPOSE OF TRIALS

Consider it pure joy, my brothers, whenever you face trials of many kinds, because you know that the testing of your faith develops perseverance. Perseverance must finish its work so that you may be mature and complete, not lacking anything. If any of you lacks wisdom, he should ask God, who gives generously to all without finding fault, and it will be given to him....

The brother in humble circumstances ought to take pride in his high position. But the one who is rich should take pride in his low position, because he will pass away like a wild flower. For the sun rises with scorching heat and withers the plant; its blossom falls and its beauty is destroyed. In the same way, the rich man will fade away even while he goes about his business.

Blessed is the man who perseveres under trial, because when he has stood the test, he will receive the crown of life that God has promised to those who love him (James 1:2-5, 9-12, italics added).

God allows trials to take place in our lives for specific reasons; they are not necessarily clear at the moment of suffering, but He has a plan. As Christians we do not strive for temporal success but for eternal success. Read what the apostle Paul wrote in 1 Corinthians 9:24-26:

> Do you not know that in a race all the runners run, but only one gets the prize? Run in such a way as to get the prize. Everyone who competes in the games goes into strict training. They do it to get a *crown that will not last*; but we do it to get a crown that will last forever. Therefore I do not run like a man *running aimlessly*; I do not fight like a man beating the air (italics added).

One of the most emotionally wrenching accounts in the Bible is the story of Job.

> In the land of Uz there lived a man whose name was Job. This man was blameless and upright; he feared God and shunned evil. He had seven sons and three daughters, and he owned seven thousand sheep, three thousand camels, five hundred yoke of oxen and five hundred donkeys, and had a large number of servants. He was the greatest man among all the people of the East (Job 1:1-3).

JOB'S CIRCUMSTANCES

What were Job's circumstances?

1. He was blameless and God-fearing.

2. He turned away from evil.

3. He was extremely wealthy.

Job's crisis was not a punishment, as many teach about Christian trials; *Job was blameless*.

THE TRIALS OF JOB

1. His donkeys and oxen were stolen, and some of his servants were slain by the Sabeans (Job 1:14-15).

2. His sheep and more servants were burned up by a fire from the sky (Job 1:16).

3. His camels were stolen by the Chaldeans, and more servants were slain (Job 1:17).

4. All his sons and daughters were killed when a great wind collapsed the house in which they were eating (Job 1:18-19).

5. Job developed boils over his entire body (Job 2:7).

After these events, Job's wife said to him, "Are you still holding on to your integrity? Curse God and die!" (Job 2:9).

He replied, "You are talking like a foolish woman. Shall we accept good from God, and not trouble?"

In all this, Job did not sin in what he
said (Job 2:10).

The most famous statement made by Job is in
chapter 13, verse 15: "Though he slay me, yet will I
hope in him."
What a marvelous testimony of perseverance.
Job had a solid foundation. Even if God were to
take his life, he still trusted Him. We encourage
you to read the entire book of Job and see the many
lessons he learned — lessons we can still learn today through his legacy.

PEACE IN CIRCUMSTANCES

The apostle Paul writes in Philippians 4:11-13:

I am not saying this because I am in need,
for I have learned to be content whatever
the circumstances. I know what it is to be
in need, and I know what it is to have
plenty. I have learned the secret of being
content in any and every situation,
whether well fed or hungry, whether living
in plenty or in want. I can do everything
through him who gives me strength.

Many times the lack of perspective can cause us
to lose sight of God's priorities. A bumper sticker
we have seen defines success as "He who dies with
the most toys wins." Jesus asks us a thought-
provoking question in Matthew 16:26:

What good will it be for a man if he gains
the whole world, yet forfeits his soul?

LOOK FORWARD

The worst thing you can do after a failure is to dwell on it continually. There comes a time to stop looking back and to begin looking forward.

> ...Forgetting what is behind and straining toward what is ahead, I press on toward the goal to win the prize for which God has called me heavenward in Christ Jesus (Phil. 3:13-14).

We certainly hope you have been helped by this book. If you should have further questions, feel free to call our radio talk show, Financial Boot Camp, on Saturdays from 3:00 to 6:00 P.M. EST on the USA Radio Network (1-800-877-2022).

Additionally, each Friday morning we take time to pray for individuals going through financial crisis. Send your prayer requests to:

Financial Boot Camp
520 Crown Oak Centre Drive
Longwood, FL 32750

We pray that God delivers you from your crisis and that He uses your circumstances for the building of His kingdom.

> And we know that in all things God works for the good of those who love him, who have been called according to his purpose (Rom. 8:28).

SMALL BUSINESS ADMINISTRATION FIELD OFFICES

REGION 1 (CT, MA, ME, NH, RI, VT)

Regional Office
155 Federal St., 9th Floor
Boston, MA 02110
(617) 451-2030

Connecticut

Hartford
330 Main St., 2nd Floor
Hartford, CT 06106
(203) 240-4700

Maine

Augusta
40 Western Ave., Rm. 512
Augusta, ME 04330
(207) 622-8378

Massachusetts

Boston
10 Causeway St., Rm. 265
Boston, MA 02222-1093
(617) 565-5591

Springfield
1550 Main St., Rm. 212
Springfield, MA 01103
(413) 785-0268

New Hampshire

Concord
193 N. Main St., Ste. 202
P.O. Box 1257
Concord, NH 03302-1257
(603) 225-1400

Rhode Island

Providence
380 Westminster St.,
   Rm. 511
Providence, RI 02903
(401) 528-4586

Vermont

Montpelier
87 State St., Rm. 205
Montpelier, VT 05602
(802) 828-4422

REGION 2 (NJ, NY, PR, VI)

Regional Office
26 Federal Plaza, Rm. 31-08
New York, NY 10278
(212) 264-1450

New Jersey

Camden
2600 Mt. Ephraim Ave.
Camden, NJ 08104
(609) 757-5183

Newark
60 Park Place, 4th Floor
Newark, NJ 07102
(201) 645-2434

New York

Albany
445 Broadway, Rm. 222
Albany, NY 12207
(518) 472-6300

Buffalo
111 W. Huron St., Rm. 1311
Buffalo, NY 14202
(716) 846-4301

Elmira
333 E. Water St., 4th Floor
Elmira, NY 14901
(607) 734-8130

Melville
35 Pinelawn Rd., Ste. 207W
Melville, NY 11747
(516) 454-0750

New York
26 Federal Plaza, Rm. 3100
New York, NY 10278
(212) 264-2454

Rochester
100 State St., Rm. 410
Rochester, NY 14614
(716) 263-6700

Syracuse
100 St. Clinton St.,
   Rm. 1071
Syracuse, NY 13260
(315) 423-5383

Puerto Rico

Hato Rey
Carlos Chardon Ave.,
   Rm. 691
Hato Rey, PR 00918
(809) 766-5572

FINANCIAL CPR

Virgin Islands

St. Croix
4200 United Shopping
   Plaza, Ste. 7
St. Croix, VI 00820-4487
(809) 778-5380

St. Thomas
Veterans Drive, Rm. 210
St. Thomas, VI 00802
(809) 774-8530

REGION 3 (DC, DE, MD, PA, VA, WV)

Regional Office
475 Allendale Rd., Ste. 201
King of Prussia, PA 19406
(215) 962-3700

Delaware

Wilmington
920 N. King St., Ste. 412
Wilmington, DE 19801
(302) 573-6295

District of Columbia

Washington, DC
1111 18th St. NW, 6th Floor
Washington, DC 20036
(202) 634-1500

Maryland

Baltimore
10 N. Calvert St., 3rd Floor
Baltimore, MD 21202
(410) 962-4392

Pennsylvania

Harrisburg
100 Chestnut St., Ste. 309
Harrisburg, PA 17101
(717) 782-3840

King of Prussia
475 Allendale Rd., Ste. 201
King of Prussia, PA 19406
(215) 962-3804

Pittsburgh
960 Penn Ave., 5th Floor
Pittsburgh, PA 15222
(412) 644-2780

Wilkes-Barre
20 N. Pennsylvania Ave.,
   Rm. 2327
Wilkes-Barre, PA 18702
(717) 826-6497

Virginia

Richmond
400 N. 8th St., Rm. 3015
Richmond, VA 23240
(804) 771-2400

West Virginia

Charleston
550 Eagan St., Ste. 309
Charleston, WV 25301
(304) 347-5220

Clarksburg
168 W. Main St., 5th Floor
Clarksburg, WV 26301
(304) 623-5631

REGION 4 (AL, FL, GA, KY, MS, NC, SC, TN)

Regional Office
1375 Peachtree St. NE,
    5th Floor
Atlanta, GA 30367-8102
(404) 347-2797

Alabama

Birmingham
2121 8th Ave. N., Ste. 200
Birmingham, AL 35203-2398
(205) 731-1344

Florida

Coral Gables
1320 S. Dixie Hwy., Ste. 501
Coral Gables, FL 33146-
    2911
(305) 536-5521

Jacksonville
7825 Baymeadows Way,
    Ste. 100-B
Jacksonville, FL 32256-7504
(904) 443-1906

Tampa
510 East Polk St.
Tampa, FL 33602-3945
(813) 228-2594

West Palm Beach
5601 Corporate Way,
    Ste. 402
W. Palm Beach, FL 33407-
    2044
(407) 689-3922

Georgia

Atlanta
1720 Peachtree Rd. NW,
    6th Floor
Atlanta, GA 30309
(404) 347-4749

Statesboro
52 Main St., Rm. 225
Statesboro, GA 30458
(912) 489-8719

Kentucky

Louisville
600 Dr. M. L. King Jr. Pl.,
    Rm. 188
Louisville, KY 40202
(502) 582-5971

Mississippi

Gulfport
One Hancock Plaza,
    Ste. 1001
Gulfport, MS 39501-7758
(601) 863-4449

Jackson
101 W. Capitol St., Ste. 400
Jackson, MS 39201
(601) 965-4378

North Carolina

Charlotte
200 N. College St.
Charlotte, NC 28202
(704) 344-6363

South Carolina

Columbia
1835 Assembly St., Rm. 358
Columbia, SC 29201
(803) 765-5376

Tennessee

Nashville
50 Vintage Way, Ste. 201
Nashville, TN 37228-1500
(615) 736-5881

REGION 5 (IL, IN, MI, MN, OH, WI)

Regional Office
300 South Riverside Plaza, Ste. 1975
Chicago, IL 60606-6617
(312) 353-5000

Illinois

Chicago
500 W. Madison St., Rm. 1250
Chicago, IL 60661-2511
(312) 353-4528

Springfield
511 W. Capitol St., Ste. 302
Springfield, IL 62704
(217) 492-4416

Indiana

Indianapolis
429 N. Penn. St., Ste. 100
Indianapolis, IN 46204-1873
(317) 226-7272

Michigan

Detroit
477 Michigan Ave., Rm. 515
Detroit, MI 48226
(313) 226-6075

Marquette
300 S. Front St.
Marquette, MI 49885
(906) 225-1108

Minnesota

Minneapolis
100 N. 6th St., Ste. 610
Minneapolis, MN 55403-1563
(612) 370-2324

Ohio

Cincinnati
525 Vine St., Ste. 870
Cincinnati, OH 45202
(513) 684-2814

Cleveland
1240 E. 9th St., Rm. 317
Cleveland, OH 44199
(216) 522-4180

Columbus
2 Nationwide Plaza, Ste. 1400
Columbus, OH 43215-2592
(614) 469-6860

Appendix A

Wisconsin

Madison
212 E. Washington Ave.,
   Rm. 213
Madison, WI 53703
(608) 264-5261

Milwaukee
310 W. Wisconsin Ave.,
   Ste. 400
Milwaukee, WI 53203
(414) 297-3941

REGION 6 (AR, LA, NM, OK, TX)

Regional Office
8625 King George Dr., Bldg. C
Dallas, TX 75235-3391
(214) 767-7633

Arkansas

Little Rock
2120 Riverfront Dr.,
   Ste. 100
Little Rock, AR 72202
(501) 324-5278

Louisiana

New Orleans
1661 Canal St., Ste. 2000
New Orleans, LA 70112
(504) 589-6685

Shreveport
500 Fannin St., Rm. 8A-08
Shreveport, LA 71101
(318) 226-5196

New Mexico

Albuquerque
625 Silver Ave. SW,
   Ste. 320
Albuquerque, NM 87102
(505) 766-1870

Oklahoma

Oklahoma City
200 N.W. 5th St.,
   Ste. 670
Oklahoma City, OK 73102
(405) 231-4301

Texas

Austin
300 E. 8th St., Rm. 520
Austin, TX 78701
(512) 482-5288

Corpus Christi
606 N. Carancahus,
   Ste. 1200
Corpus Christi, TX 78476
(512) 888-3331

El Paso
10737 Gateway W.,
   Ste. 320
El Paso, TX 79935
(915) 540-5676

Fort Worth
819 Taylor St.,
   Rm. 8A-27
Fort Worth, TX 76102
(817) 334-3777

FINANCIAL CPR

Fort Worth
4300 Amon Carter Blvd.,
 Ste. 114
Fort Worth, TX 76155
(817) 885-6500

Harlingen
222 E. Van Buren St.,
 Rm. 500
Harlingen, TX 78550
(512) 427-8533

Houston
9301 Southwest Freeway,
 Ste. 550
Houston, TX 77074-1591
(713) 773-6500

Lubbock
1611 Tenth St., Ste. 200
Lubbock, TX 79401
(806) 743-7462

Marshall
505 E. Travis, Rm. 103
Marshall, TX 75670
(903) 935-5257

San Antonio
7400 Blanco Rd., Ste. 200
San Antonio, TX 78216
(512) 229-4535

REGION 7 (IA, KS, MO, NE)

Regional Office
911 Walnut St., 13th Floor
Kansas City, MO 64106
(816) 426-3608

Iowa

Cedar Rapids
373 Collins Rd. NE,
 Rm. 100
Cedar Rapids, IA 52402-
 3147
(319) 393-8630

Des Moines
210 Walnut St., Rm. 749
Des Moines, IA 50309
(515) 284-4422

Kansas

Wichita
100 E. English St.,
 Ste. 510
Wichita, KS 67202
(316) 269-6273

Missouri

Kansas City
323 W. 8th St., Ste. 501
Kansas City, MO 64105
(816) 374-6708

Springfield
620 S. Glenstone St.,
 Ste. 110
Springfield, MO 65802-3200
(417) 864-7670

St. Louis
815 Olive St., Rm. 242
St. Louis, MO 63101
(314) 539-6600

Appendix A

Nebraska

Omaha
11145 Mill Valley Rd.
Omaha, NE 68154
(402) 221-4691

REGION 8 (CO, MT, ND, SD, UT, WY)

Regional Office
999 18th St.,
   Ste. 701
Denver, CO 80202
(303) 294-7186

Colorado

Denver
721 19th St., Rm. 407
Denver, CO 80201-0660
(303) 844-3984

Montana

Helena
301 S. Park,
   Rm. 528
Helena, MT 59626
(406) 449-5381

North Dakota

Fargo
657 Second Ave. N,
   Rm. 218
Fargo, ND 58108-3086
(701) 239-5131

South Dakota

Sioux Falls
101 S. Main Ave.,
   Ste. 101
Sioux Falls, SD 57102-0527
(605) 330-4231

Utah

Salt Lake City
125 S. State St.,
   Rm. 2237
Salt Lake City, UT 84138-1195
(801) 524-5804

Wyoming

Casper
100 East B St., Rm. 4001
Casper, WY 82602-2839
(307) 261-5761

REGION 9 (AZ, CA, GU, HI, NV)

Regional Office
71 Stevens St.
San Francisco, CA 94105-2939
(415) 744-6402

Arizona

Phoenix
2828 N. Central Ave.,
   Ste. 800
Phoenix, AZ 85004-1025
(602) 640-2316

FINANCIAL CPR

Tucson
300 W. Congress St.,
  Rm. 7-H
Tucson, AZ 85701-1319
(602) 670-6715

California

Fresno
2719 North Air Fresno Dr.
Fresno, CA 93727-1547
(209) 487-5189

Glendale
330 N. Brand Blvd.
Glendale, CA 91203
(213) 894-2956

Sacramento
660 J St., Rm. 215
Sacramento, CA 95814
(916) 551-1426

San Diego
880 Front St.,
  Rm. 238 4-S-29
San Diego, CA 92188
(619) 557-7252

San Francisco
211 Main St., 4th Floor
San Francisco, CA 94105-
  1988
(415) 744-6820

Santa Ana
901 W. Civic Ctr. Dr.,
  Ste. 160
Santa Ana, CA 92703-2352
(714) 836-2494

Ventura
6477 Telephone Rd., Ste. 10
Ventura, CA 93003-4459
(805) 642-1866

Guam

Agana
238 Archbishop F.C.
Flores St., Rm. 508
Agana, GU 96910
(671) 472-7277

Hawaii

Honolulu
300 Ala Moana, Rm. 2213
Honolulu, HI 96850-4981
(808) 541-2990

Nevada

Las Vegas
301 E. Steward St., Rm. 301
Las Vegas, NV 89125-2527
(702) 388-6611

Reno
50 S. Virginia St., Rm. 238
Reno, NV 89505-3216
(702) 784-5268

REGION 10 (AK, ID, OR, WA)

Regional Office
2615 4th Ave., Rm. 440
Seattle, WA 98121
(206) 553-5676

Appendix A

Alaska

Anchorage
222 W. 8th Ave., Rm. 67
Anchorage, AK 99513-7559
(901) 271-4022

Idaho

Boise
1020 Main St., Ste. 290
Boise, ID 83702-5745
(208) 334-1696

Oregon

Portland
222 S.W. Columbia, Ste. 522
Portland, OR 97201-6605
(503) 326-2682

Washington

Seattle
915 Second Ave., Rm. 1791
Seattle, WA 98174-1088
(206) 553-1420

Spokane
W. 601 First Ave., 10th Floor
Spokane, WA 99204-0317
(509) 353-2800

RESOURCES

Banking Problems

Federal Deposit Insurance Corporation
Office of Consumer Affairs
550 17th St. NW, Rm. F-130
Washington, DC 20429
(202) 898-3536
(800) 934-FDIC

Comptroller of the Currency
Compliance Management
U.S. Department of the Treasury
250 E St. SW
Washington, DC 20219
(202) 874-4820

Office of Thrift Supervision
U.S. Department of the Treasury
1700 G St. NW
Washington, DC 20552
(202) 906-6000

Garnishment of Wages

Wage and Hour Division
Fair Labor Standards
U.S. Department of Labor
200 Constitution Ave. NW, Rm. S3516
Washington, DC 20210
(202) 219-7043

U.S. Department of Labor
local offices

Housing Discrimination

Fair Housing Enforcement Division
Office of Fair Housing and Equal
  Opportunity
U.S. Department of Housing and Urban
  Development
451 7 St. SW
Washington, DC 20410
(800) 669-9777

Job Discrimination

Equal Employment Opportunity Commission
1801 L St. NW
Washington, DC 20507
(800) 669-4000

Real Estate Agents and Brokers

State Real Estate Commissions
local offices

BIBLIOGRAPHY

Allen, Robert. *Nothing Down*. New York: Simon & Schuster, 1984.

Blanchard, Kenneth, and William Onken. *The One-Minute Manager Meets the Monkey*. New York: Simon & Schuster, 1988.

Covey, Stephen R. *The Seven Habits of Highly Effective People*. New York: Simon & Schuster, 1989.

Dawson, Kenneth, and Sheryl. *Job Search: The Total System*. New York: John Wiley & Sons, 1988.

Dicks, J.W. *30 Day Quick Start*. Orlando: J.W. Dicks Research Institute, 1992.

Eisenson, Marc. *The Banker's Secret*. New York: Villard Books, 1991.

Fisk, Asa. *You're Hired*. Houston: Merechip Publishing Company, 1992.

Haman, Edward. *How to File Your Own Bankruptcy*. Clearwater, Fla.: Sphinx Publishing, 1992.

Hansel, Tim. *When I Relax I Feel Guilty*. Elgin: Ill.: David C. Cook, 1979.

Lesko, Matthew. *Lesko's Info-Power*. Kensington, Md.: Info USA, 1990.

Mackay, Harvey. *How to Swim With the Sharks Without Being Eaten Alive*. New York: Morrow, William, & Co., 1988.

Nichol, Gudrun. *Debtor's Rights and Duties*. Clearwater, Fla.: Sphinx Publishing, 1992.

Pilot, Kevin. *Credit Approved*. Holbrook, Mass.: Bob Adams, Inc., 1992.

Polto, Pearl. *Pearl Polto's Easy Guide to Good Credit*. New York: Berkley Publishing Group, 1990.

Summers, Mark. *Bankruptcy Explained*. New York: John Wiles & Sons, 1989.

Warda, Mark. *Landlord Rights and Duties*. Clearwater, Fla.: Sphinx Publishing, 1991.

PRODUCTS AND SERVICES OFFERED BY FINANCIAL BOOT CAMP

Our goal is to make available financial information which will answer your questions and help you be a better steward of the money God has given you. We will be happy to send you, as one of our readers, a free copy of our monthly newsletter. Please phone 1-800-829-4037.

The American Dream
$16.95 + $4 shipping and handling

Jim Paris teams up with attorney J. W. Dicks to help consumers attain their financial goals. Hardcover book addresses ten proven principles for financial freedom.

Boot Camp Three-Night Seminar
$39.95 + $4 shipping and handling

Experience Jim Paris's live TV seminar on three one-hour videos. Jim teaches proper financial stewardship principles found in Matthew 25.

Estate Planning
$19.95 + $4 shipping and handling

In this video Jim explains the value of proper estate planning in easy-to-understand, non-technical language.

Financial Boot Camp for Single Christians
$9.95 + $4 shipping and handling

One-hour audio tape to help single Christians of all ages survive the economically turbulent times.

Financial Boot Camp Software
$49.00 + $4 shipping and handling

Financial Boot Camp software makes it simple and easy to handle your financial and investment needs properly. With it you can access accounting functions, check writing, budget creation and maintenance, mortgage amortization schedules, financial calculating and investment guidelines.

How to Drive a Real Bargain
$39.95 + $4 shipping and handling

Have you always wondered why some people get a good deal on cars and others don't? Jim Paris and former car salesman James Ross team up to teach you the *art of dealing with car salesmen*. Course includes three books and three cassettes.

Inside Boot Camp
$15.00 + $4 shipping and handling

One-hour audio cassette detailing Jim's most popular strategies — from obtaining low interest rate credit cards to investing with no commission. A must for beginners.

The Insurance Shopping Network
$24.95

Are you looking for the best rates on term life and health insurance coverage for you and your family? Stop! Look no further. The typical Christian consumer is sold insurance without ever getting quotes from other qualified carriers. That is why Jim Paris designed the *Insurance Shopping Network* to do just that — shop from a national network of qualified carriers to provide you, the consumer, with the best coverage available. The *Insurance Shopping Network* does not sell insurance — it simply scans our nearly limitless database to search for your coverage needs at the lowest price. If we cannot find you the best rates on life and/or health insurance coverage, we will refund your money.

Lighten Your Pack
$15.00 + $4 shipping and handling

A Christian's guide to lowering tax burdens morally, ethically and legally. One-hour audio cassette.

Mutual Fund Investing for the '90s
$9.95 + $4 shipping and handling

Did you know there are now over three thousand mutual funds in America? In this one-hour cassette tape Jim will teach you how to invest with no commission, get started investing with just one dollar and much, much more!

Paris Perspective Newsletter
$67.00 per year

Now you can stay on the cutting edge of personal finance with the new *Paris Perspective* newsletter. Every month Jim Paris will provide you with his insights on topics such as mutual fund investing and getting the best deal on a new car. If you are a concerned Christian consumer looking for an "edge" in finance and investment, the *Paris Perspective* is for you.

Special Forces Training — Credit and Debt
$44.95 + $4 shipping and handling

Jim Paris has compiled a program for Christian consumers who are struggling with debt or bad credit. Three one-hour audio tapes *plus* two books — Pearl Polto's *Easy Guide to Good Credit* and Mark Eisenson's *The Banker's Secret* — provide you with the proper tools to lower debt effectively and repair bad or nonexistent credit ratings.

The Survival System
$99.00 + $5 shipping and handling

The complete training course in personal finance from Financial Boot Camp. A must for the Christian consumer who is committed to living God's plan for financial stewardship. Includes six one-hour audio tapes plus 120 pages of reference material.

*For more information or to order
any of the products or services listed,
please call or write:*

Financial Boot Camp for Christians
520 Crown Oak Centre Drive
Longwood, FL 32750
1-800-829-4037

Visa/MasterCard, American Express
and Discover cards accepted.

*Florida residents,
please add 7 percent sales tax.*

If you enjoyed *Financial CPR*,
we would like to recommend
the following books:

Financial Boot Camp
by James L. Paris
This best-seller is a guide to avoiding
fifteen consumer land mines.
Full of practical information and valuable
resource material, *Financial Boot Camp*
will teach you how to establish a good credit rating,
become a home owner, slash your taxes and more.
Author James L. Paris is heard each week
on radio stations throughout the country and is known
as the "Christian Consumer Advocate."

The American Dream
by J. W. Dicks and James L. Paris
To help you achieve your American dream,
authors J. W. Dicks and James L. Paris
have written a powerful book —
*The American Dream: Ten Proven
Principles for Financial Freedom.*
By following these principles,
you will be able to take control of your life,
your finances and your dreams.

Available at your local Christian
bookstore or from:

Creation House
600 Rinehart Road
Lake Mary, FL 32746
1-800-451-4598